PIONEERS
Thoughts on Global Design Research

Megan Anderson, Geke van Dijk & Bas Raijmakers / STBY

in collaboration with Kat Gough, Michael Davis Burchat and the Reach Network

Pioneers: Thoughts on Global Design Research

Editorial Team: Megan Anderson, Geke van Dijk
and Bas Raijmakers (STBY)
Co-authors: Kat Gough, Michael Davis Burchat
Contributors: Quicksand, Apogee, fuelfor,
Matchboxology
Copy editor: Sophie Knight, Daphne Stylianou
Graphic design: Hyperkit
Printed by: Swallowtail
Edition: 700

All images by STBY and Reach partners, unless otherwise
noted on page 96

Publisher:
STBY Ltd.
221–222 Shoreditch High Street
London E1 6PJ
United Kingdom
www.stby.eu
info@stby.eu

ISBN: 978-1-5272-0940-4

Pioneers: Thoughts on Global Design Research was made
possible in part by support from Innovate UK, the UK's
Innovation Agency.

..STBY...

Innovate UK
Technology Strategy Board

Reach

PREFACE

As the world becomes flatter, in the words of Thomas Friedman[1], more organisations must take the local and global into account when thinking about strategy and innovation. This sounds straightforward and sensible, but how do enterprises actually organise, strategise and design new products and services amidst the forces of globalisation? There is, of course, no one-size-fits-all approach to operating successfully on a global scale and many organisations find themselves constantly grappling with these issues.

The Japanese term *dochakuka*, which means the adaptation of farming techniques to local conditions, was first used to describe 'global localisation'. That concept has since been popularised in its portmanteau form, *glocalisation*, to refer to the way in which organisations have adapted to designing products and services at a global scale, while being sensitive to local considerations like language, laws, policies, norms and customs. The McDonald's menu is often cited as one of the most straightforward illustrations of this phenomenon, though there are seemingly countless more elaborate examples.

At STBY we have been exploring issues like this for many years through our own practice as part of a wider global network of design research agencies called Reach, alongside our work with globally operating clients. Partly as a natural response to a demand for globally networked design research, and partly motivated by a shared desire among partner organisations to work and learn together, the Reach Network has grown organically over time. Growth, here, refers not only to partner numbers, but also to collective knowledge, shared resources and network offerings.

Pioneers is a collection of reflections on global design research, co-funded by STBY and Innovate UK, and written in collaboration with Reach partners across the globe. Our stories and insights are derived from real-world cases and hands-on experiences of working on global design research projects over the past eight years. The title is inspired by a largely unexplored and ill-defined field that we refer to as 'global design research'. In this sense we find the language of pioneers and adventurers fitting metaphors to explain what have, at times, been very emergent, ad-hoc ways of working. After years of doing and reflecting upon global design research projects, we are happy to have the opportunity to consolidate our thoughts and critically reflect on the past, present and future of global design research practice. We hope that this publication will inspire and enable designers, researchers, strategists and innovation managers working with and within global organisations.

1   Friedman, T. (2005). The World Is Flat. A Brief History of
     the Twenty-First Century. Farrar, Straus and Giroux.

We are here

Pale Blue Dot is a photograph of planet Earth taken
on February 14, 1990, by the Voyager 1 space probe
from a distance of about 6 billion kilometers. In the
centre of the photograph, Earth's apparent size is less
than a pixel; the planet appears as a tiny dot against
the vastness of space. Popularised by astronomer and
author, Carl Sagan, the photograph continues to inspire
wonderment and global togetherness.

It may be in the cultural particularities of people — in their oddities — that some of the most instructive revelations of what it is to be generically human are to be found. Clifford Geertz

ABOUT STBY

STBY is a design research consultancy specialised in design research for service innovation. Based in London and Amsterdam, our creative research projects connect organisations with the lives and experiences of their customers. This helps our clients in industry and the public sector to innovate their service offering, adding value to both their customers and the organisation. Our projects generate rich, visually illustrated and engaging materials, that bring real people into the heart of service innovation processes. STBY is the initiator and co-founder of the REACH network. www.stby.eu

ABOUT THE REACH NETWORK

Reach is a network of highly skilled and experienced companies around the world with a deep expertise in design research. Our experience in both design and customer research enables us to seamlessly integrate our research activities in design and innovation processes. The partners in the Reach network are seasoned professionals who are truly grounded in their local culture. This facilitates faster, cheaper, and more effective international collaborations than those possible via traditional models for international consumer research. www.globaldesignresearch.com

Several partners of the Reach network contributed to this publication:
Quicksand (New Delhi, Bangalore and Goa, India)
Apogee (Hong Kong, China)
fuelfor (Singapore, and Barcelona, Spain)
Matchboxology (Cape Town and Johannesburg, South Africa)

ABOUT THE EDITORS

Megan Anderson
Megan Anderson is a Design Researcher at STBY in London. She is a passionate advocate for the use of service design and design research within the public sector. She is also a PhD candidate at Leiden University. Her academic research explores how public sector organisations design and improve new and existing services. Originally from Singapore, Megan has lived and worked in Australia, The Netherlands and the United Kingdom.

Geke van Dijk
Geke is co-founder and Strategy Director of STBY in London and Amsterdam. She has a background in ethnographic research, user-centered design and services marketing. She is passionate about exploring the ways people actively co-produce their customer journeys by picking and mixing from multi-channel service touch points. Geke regularly publishes, presents and teaches on Service Design and Design Research. She is the initiator and chair of the Service Design Network Netherlands, and an active member of the international Service Design Network. Geke holds a PhD in Computer Sciences from the Open University in the UK, co-supervised by the Business School of the OU.

Bas Raijmakers
Bas is co-founder and Creative Director of STBY in London and Amsterdam. He has a background in Cultural Studies, the internet industry and interaction design. His main passion is to bring the people for whom we design into design and innovation processes, using visual storytelling. He holds a PhD in Design Interactions from the Royal College of Art in London. He is also a Professor in Strategic Creativity at Design Academy Eindhoven.

ABOUT THE CO-AUTHORS

Kat Gough
co-author of the chapter on 'Practice'
Kat is Design Director at Kitchen Table Design Research in London. She is passionate about the principles and practice of inclusive design, as a way to ensure products and services are meeting the needs of as many users as possible. Kitchen Table provides specialist research and service design skills to organisations, such as inclusive design, co-design, portfolio planning and design research. She works across the public sector and industry. Kat previously worked as Head of Ethnographic Research for Nokia Design in London.

Michael Davis Burchat
co-author of the chapter on 'Practice'
Michael is founder and director of Big Human in Toronto. Michael's work introduces human-centred reasoning as a practical way to reorient profit-and-loss decision making and create value for people. His prior work in the domains of corporate strategy, design strategy, consumer insights, business-process design and concept making, and industrial design enables him to bridge silos with design thinking.Michael previously worked as Portfolio Roadmap Manager and Design Strategy Manager for Nokia in Helsinki and Beijing.

A special thank you to
Myrtille Danze, Andreas Sommerwerk, Katie Tzanidou and Tomer Sharon for the great conversations about the new frontiers of global design research; Sam Miller who contributed to some of the copy editing when she was still part of the STBY team; All our clients, partners and friends around the world who have inspired, motivated and challenged us over the years.

CONTENTS

THE EVOLUTION OF DESIGN RESEARCH

STBY, our wider community of partners and clients, fully work today in the area of global design research. We all have intimate knowledge of its daily practice, and we understand each other well when we talk about the underlying principles. Sometimes we almost forget how relatively young this 'discipline' is in the creative industry, and how much we are pioneering and cultivating it as we go. This was the stimulus for this publication. We felt it would be good to create a focus point for joint reflection on state-of-the-art global design research, so we can collectively strengthen our understanding of where global design research has come from, what it is now, and where we see it heading in the coming years. We also hope it offers other peers in the field an opportunity to join this reflection and discussion, so together we can keep pioneering and developing the field.

Design research did not come out of nowhere. In academia it has existed for over 50 years, and has shifted its attention a few times — from trying to understand the rules designers follow when they design, to using design methods as a way to create academic knowledge. In industry, which we focus on in this publication, design research has evolved whilst standing on the shoulders of many other fields beyond design itself: for example, engineering, anthropology, business innovation and industrial design, to name but a few. Though the term 'design research' has been around for more than five decades in academia, and has taken on several meanings since the start, it consolidated in the practice of creative industries only in the last decade, as a term for research that supports innovation through the use of design methods as a way to create insights and opportunities. Now many creative agencies do design research as part of their design-driven innovation practices, but ten years ago, one had to look hard to find the few that were pioneering: Doblin, E-lab, IDEO and several research labs from tech giants like Microsoft, Intel and Apple among them. Some had been pioneering already for many years. Design research, as it is known in industry today, has many roots, sparked by simultaneous catalysing developments in society, business and technology such as digitisation, open innovation and the self-service economy.

Design has gradually evolved over the years from making stuff and then testing it, to integrating user research as input in the design process, which often proved to result in better outcomes. Inspired by the boost that the second World War gave to ergonomic design of military equipment, designers in the 1950s began to recognise the use of ergonomics to inform their designs, and this encouraged them to take a closer look at how people make use of things, mostly with the perspective of physical measurements (e.g. the perfect height for a table, or the perfect grip for the steering wheel in a car).

The emergence of ergonomics helped designers to better consider how people actually made use of the things they designed — from how they use their hands to how big their hands actually are. Eventually this led to the introduction of standard measurements of people, which were introduced through the archetypes of 'Joe' and 'Josephine' in Dreyfuss' book Designing for People (1955), and which remain central to ergonomics. However, when read in detail, you can see that not all of it is about purely 'technical' measurements. Some of the considerations are about cultural differences, such as whether someone could be expected to wear heavy winter gloves, or the varying length of female fingernails.

When products started to become interactive in the 1980s and designers needed to anticipate how people would make use of new and complex electronic equipment (such as computers, copiers, video recorders), theories and frameworks from cognitive psychology proved to be very helpful. This led to the rise of usability research in industry in the 1990s, with Jakob Nielsen[2] as its most prominent representative in industry. Usability research at this time, however, was mostly lab-based, and did not take into account the rich contexts in which these interactions between people and electronic machines took place.

Although the first ethnographers were hired into design as early as in the 1970s, they were exceptions. Rick Robinson for Doblin and later E-lab was a pioneer of early-stage ethnographic research in design[3]. The interest in context grew stronger over time — for instance, through the emergence of 'human-centred design', which considers people and their activities in context. When people started

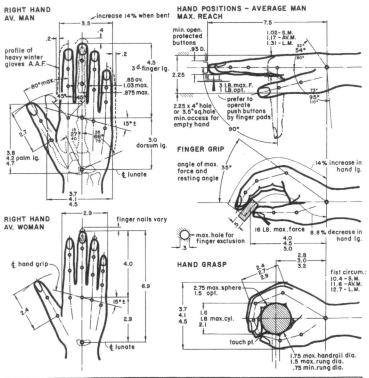

HAND MEASUREMENTS OF MEN, WOMEN AND CHILDREN

HAND DATA	MEN			WOMEN			CHILDREN			
	2.5 %tile	50.%tile	97.5 %tile	2.5 %tile	50.%tile	97.5 %tile	6 yr.	8 yr.	11 yr.	14 yr.
hand length	6.8	7.5	8.2	6.2	6.9	7.5	5.1	5.6	6.3	7.0
hand breadth	3.2	3.5	3.8	2.6	2.9	3.1	2.3	2.5	2.8	—
3d. finger lg.	4.0	4.5	5.0	3.6	4.0	4.4	2.9	3.2	3.5	4.0
dorsum lg.	2.8	3.0	3.2	2.6	2.9	3.1	2.2	2.4	2.8	3.0
thumb length	2.4	2.7	3.0	2.2	2.4	2.6	1.8	2.0	2.2	2.4

The emergence of ergonomics helped designers to better consider how people actually made use of the things they designed — from how they use their hands to how big their hands actually are. Eventually this led to the introduction of standard measurements of people, which were introduced through the archetypes of 'Joe' and 'Josephine' in Dreyfuss' book Designing for People (1955[1]), and which remain central to ergonomics. However, when read in detail, you can see that not all of it is about purely 'technical' measurements. Some of the considerations are about cultural differences, such as whether someone could be expected to wear heavy winter gloves, or the varying length of female fingernails.

to carry their technological devices with them and also share them with others (such as mobile phones), the variety in context of use for devices grew and became more important for designers to consider. This raised an interest in the theory and practice of contextual inquiry methods from the fields of anthropology, sociology, and cultural studies. Big tech companies like Apple and Intel started hiring ethnographers from the mid-1990s. Design companies like Philips Design and IDEO also started to bring contextual research methods into their work at that time.

In parallel, user-experience research emerged in the 1990s as a response to the purely functional focus of usability research, demonstrating that emotion is also important in how people use devices[4]. Participatory design, meanwhile, emerged in Scandinavia as a concrete way to collaborate with the people you design for. These turns to context, experience and participation are all still important strands in design research in industry today.

One additional turn was added this century. As it became clear over the past 15 years that many products are actually part of larger product-service systems, and that these systems allow people a large freedom to choose how and when to make use of a product or service, the research that informs design in industry had to evolve further again, to describe this active and empowered use by people in the design process in much more holistic ways than had been done before. Ethnographic methods offered a framework in

Design research in context using ethnographic methods
creates a very different picture of people than
ergonomics or usability tests do. Here Apogee, the
Hong Kong based Reach partner of STBY, observes,
interviews and films a participant in the Shanghai
Metro. The participant is at the centre, with a focus
on what she does. Jo Wong films how the participant
interacts with her phone, while asking her questions
in Cantonese. Dan Szuc films the participant, while
keeping an eye on what else in the context might be
worth filming because it could make a meaningful
contribution to the story she is telling.

which people's real-life activities and motivations could be placed at the forefront of the design process of multi-touchpoint ecosystems. People's use of these systems is often described in 'journeys' that combine products, services and systems into one experience. This approach is by now widely known as 'service design'. Today hardly any service design project gets off the ground without any ethnographically-inspired exploratory research (often called design research) in the early stages, as well as more market- and usability-focused validation research in the later stages of the service design process.

Another reason for the growing relevance of people- and context-focused design research for service design over the past 10 years has been that service design projects (or service innovation projects, as we sometimes prefer to call them), have become so complex and interdisciplinary that not placing people squarely in the middle of the design process would make it difficult to find a common reference point for all the various specialists involved. When we say 'people', we mean both intended users, customers, and citizens, as well as the people who are likely to deliver the services.

Without that common reference point to calibrate priorities and scope, the team would struggle to take informed decisions on concepts and implementations. Many different experts from all sorts of disciplines need to collaborate in this process of ongoing refinement (e.g. product design, visual design, interaction design, software development, business strategy, marketing, communications, human resources, policy, etc.). All these experts are involved in an intricate staged process of interdisciplinary co-design. By providing shared reference points on directions and ambitions, design research has evolved into one of the key pillars of service innovation, and increasingly business strategy. The roots of design research in participatory design have certainly helped to develop this position for design research: apart from collecting data in the field and making sense of it, design research also learned how to orchestrate activities[5], such as workshops, that create insights, opportunities, and even ideas together with other disciplines.

Converging trends in adjacent fields

Design research has also been influenced by a gradual evolution in the field of humanities research. Whereas long ago social researchers were mostly analytical investigators who placed themselves comfortably outside of the design process, they have learned over time to appreciate being part of the design process and to actively contribute to the outcomes. Over the decades, various connections between design and social research have been identified and explored by pioneers. They have been nudging the emerging field of design research forward. Rather than just observing and often criticising things from the outside, social researchers are now more likely to join design teams and contribute to a design or innovation process and its outcomes.

Of course not all research that is somehow related to design and innovation should now immediately be seen as 'design research'. There is, for instance, still the traditional field of marketing research. This usually takes place outside of the design and innovation process. It usually happens either before (e.g. trend research, or business analysis) or after (e.g. customer satisfaction surveys). For a business, this type of research can still be very useful and certainly highly valuable, but it has a different purpose and different character than design research, and it will therefore be commissioned at different times.

Furthermore, simultaneous evolutions in society coincided with and strengthened the gradual converging developments in design and research. As consumers, citizens, travellers, students, employees, and so on are becoming better informed, well equipped and more mobile, they are becoming more empowered and are demanding high quality services and interactions from organisations. People nowadays are very active and resourceful. They expect to be taken seriously, and rightly so. Organisations, whether they are operating in the corporate or public sector, need to actively engage with their target groups. They cannot simply lean back and assume they know what's best for everyone. They need to be open and transparent, and engage with the people they work with and serve. Design research can play an important role in this dynamic process by exploring and relaying needs, preferences, passions, concerns, and opportunities.

This leads us nicely to another simultaneous evolution, and that is the one happening in the world of service providers. Whether they are businesses, public sector or non profit, all of them have learned, or are still learning, to open up and engage more actively with their audiences. One of the effects of this is that many organisations have now complemented their traditional secretive in-house R&D with open innovation initiatives that put interactions with the audience and other external stakeholders right in the centre. Words like co-creation, collaboration and partnerships are more common in this context now than before. And the same for terminology such as 'design thinking', 'service design', and 'ethnographic research'. On a strategic level, organisations are starting to use this more and more as a frame of reference. Part of this development is due to design research showing the way, and at the same time this development is also nudging design research to further develop itself as a strategic resource. The service economy was not invented by service design, but the successful application and added value of the human-centered and design-led approach of service design has been elemental in its acceptance by C-level business people. This is largely due to the open and collaborative approach people-centred designers and researchers bring to the table.

And finally, a simultaneous evolution has been taking place in technology as well. Traditionally developments in technology would largely move from R&D to detailed production, then shipping, and then (market) testing, in a so-called 'technology push' approach to innovation. Nowadays even technology-driven innovation in many startups is more likely to be an iterative and lean development[6] that moves from early stage explorations with target groups, to several rounds of prototyping and testing, to a 'minimal viable product' that can be launched and further developed based on real-time testing and evaluation. Design research caters for this agile and interdisciplinary process by teaming up with the other disciplines involved, and by supporting every stage in the process. Design research has a role in helping to find answers to both short-term questions from development teams and more long-term overarching questions from strategy teams. When done in a well-planned and structured way, the data generated can even be used across multiple projects, and can therefore deliver much more return on investment than traditional, strongly focused research.

Today, we can confidently say that human- and context-focused research, building on a range of social research disciplines, is firmly and comfortably integrated in many design processes. Many design teams and designers, as well as the organisations they work in, have wholeheartedly integrated this type of research as a natural part of their design activities. Moreover, the discipline of design research is becoming widely acknowledged and accepted in adjacent related fields such as business, technology, and the public sector.

STBY, alongside many other pioneering peers around the globe, has contributed to this gradual development since the start of this century. This has been, and still is, an iterative process in which we act and learn as reflective practitioners[7]. Having two feet firmly on the ground in the ambitious and fast-evolving practice of service innovation on the market, and also regularly sticking our heads in the more academic clouds of reflection on methodology and broader meanings of our work, has helped us in compiling and shaping this publication.

1   Dreyfuss, H. (1955). *Designing for People*. New York, Simon and Schuster.
2   Nielsen, J. (1994). *Usability Engineering*. Morgan Kaufmann.
3   Koskinen, I. et al. (2012). *Design Research Through Practice: From the field, lab and showroom*. Waltham, MA; Morgan Kaufman.
4   Jordan, P. (2000). *Designing Pleasurable Products: An Introduction to the New Human Factors*. CRC Press.
5   Raijmakers, B., Vervloed, J., Jan Wierda, K. (2015). Orchestration. *CRISP Magazine n.5 2015*: pp. 24-33.
6   Reis, E. (2011). *The Lean Startup*. Penguin Books Ltd.
7   Schön, D. (1983). *The Reflective Practitioner*. Basic Books.

NEW FRONTIERS FOR GLOBAL DESIGN RESEARCH

We are in the middle of the development of global design research today, and together with others in the field, we have come a long way already. It is always good to acknowledge and celebrate what the wider global design research community has achieved. But on the other hand we would not be pioneers if we were not also already looking at new frontiers to explore. What motivates us in terms of new challenges? What do we expect from the future?

Connecting the global and the local

In international design research there are often 'global' observations that are made across people and locations, and 'local' observations that are only made for specific people or specific contexts. It is not uncommon to make similar observations in Bangalore, Shanghai, Barcelona and London; we all live in a global world, we are all human, and technology is connecting us all more and more every day. In whatever locale you do design research, the global will be present. But the local flavour and details are also always present. There are always some observations that may be unique to the local context you are in.

The combination of global and local observations does not however automatically lead to a similar division between global and local insights. Through analysis, in our

> The problem I have with globalisation is that it can also mean ignoring the local for the sake of efficiency. Economically it makes a lot of sense to think globally, because you can scale things more easily. While this is a valid approach from an economic perspective, I feel it tends to ignore local insights and needs. This can also make the world more boring, because you create less local diversity. Andreas Sommerwerk

case with the different local design research teams and client teams together, observations across locations must be interpreted to arrive at global and local insights. This is a craft that the global design research community can still polish further, and with STBY and Reach we are keen to contribute with some crucial understanding of this craft that we see further developing over the coming years.

We focus on meaningful local differences that truly merit the formulation of a separate local insight. All other insights could be globally relevant and applicable. Meaningful here means that it makes sense from the perspective of the participants in the research as well as the design researchers from the different locations involved. Being this frugal with allowing local insights to come out of the analysis allows our clients, organisations and teams that operate internationally to connect the global and the local in a practical and efficient way.

Connecting the global and the local in this practical yet meaningful way is still largely a green field. In our current practice we have found an approach to this that seems to work, but it can surely be developed much further. Also, with global culture developing at great speed, this is an area where ongoing interpretation and analysis are needed. What global culture means to people around the world, and what it offers them, plays into this and will have to be part of pushing the craft of creating and connecting global and local insights further.

> When there is an expectation that a certain market will be more welcoming for a product, it's important to understand that market first before anything else. Or there may be certain top countries with the most users for a particular product. If that is the core of your audience, you better understand what their pain points are, or what the cultural differences are that you need to be aware of. In these cases local investigations are more uniquely focused and targeted. Katie Tzanidou

In some places I hire a local design research agency and work very closely with them. When you go to China or Japan you simply have to do that — you don't speak the language, you don't know the culture, you don't even know how to find people to speak with. But when it is in Memphis, Tennessee which is very different from NY, I would not consider to hire a local vendor, we would just go on our own. We are trying to see what the threshold is — when do we do it alone, and when do we partner with local vendors? It is not easy to figure this out. Tomer Sharon

In many ways it is key people in the organisation who connect the global and local. This is often taken for granted. It is not consciously managed, it is mostly intuitive. When organisations grow from a locally based organisation to a global organisation, they'll put people in charge who are locals with lots of international experience, or foreigners who have a connection to that particular local base of the organisation and have worked across a few locations. These types of people are able to bridge cultural differences. This constant bridging requires different sensitivities and different experiences. It enables people to make connections across different levels. Over the years I have seen that the involvement of local people in this is clearly growing. Myrtille Danse

We are constantly having conversations in our team about whether we should make an effort to go out and learn more about people's needs and preferences in a particular location. And of course, yes we should, but it is often a difficult decision, because you need to take choices and set priorities, and you simply cannot do it all. Even just doing research all around the US is something huge, let alone around the world. About 60% of our customer base is outside of the US, so we are doing research in many different places, but not everywhere all the time. Tomer Sharon

We often see people from Europe or America coming to developing countries and talking about these creative and innovative tools and methods – 'design thinking', 'co-creation' and such – and it's interesting, but it's naturally hard to relate to when it refers to another context and it has come from somewhere else. It's often difficult to implement, because you do not have many people in the local community who are familiar with this way of thinking and working. What we have had to do very often is take an approach that has been developed in a Western or European context and "tropicalise" it – using local examples and local language, before linking it to things in the local context so you make it more understandable and relatable. Then it becomes more relevant. Myrtille Danse

The focus on global or local varies from project to project, depending on how mature a product is. Sometimes there is already a lot of knowledge about a local market where a current product is based in. Things are pretty clear then, and easy to access from a logistical point of view. This gives a good basis to go out and explore other markets. You get the fundamentals right, and then you explore what is further away. With that baseline, you can find out if needs or behaviours are different in other places. In this model it is relatively easy to connect the dots between various localities. Katie Tzanidou

We provide office spaces around the world, but our offering is not just office space, it is also the connection to other people. One thing we have found is that you can copy and paste a lot of office design elements from one location to the other. The challenge however, is to connect to specific cultural preferences that people locally have in using the space. These can be surprisingly different. For instance, in NY everyone tends to go out for lunch, but in Amsterdam people prefer to bring their lunch from home, put it in the fridge, and then all have their lunch at the same time. Our challenge was not so much in providing the fridges, that is easy, but in providing enough common space to make those group lunches possible. There are many examples of where our standard design templates did not work. The company needed to suffer a bit to understand this, but in the end it did, and now we are more sensitive to this. It is our job to understand those differences. Tomer Sharon

Pushing the boundaries of global collaboration

Although inspiring and fulfilling, thinking and working globally can be quite challenging. Multiple languages, time zones and ways of working can easily get in the way of smooth progress throughout any global project. During years of experiencing this and learning on the fly, we have established some routines and principles for how to deal with some of these issues, but with the international community of pioneers in design research we are also still in the process of figuring this out, and there is much more to experiment with and learn from. The field of global design research has not settled on a preferred approach to global collaboration yet, and probably never will. We can definitely learn from each other's ways of working.

Two ways of doing global design research seem to be already quite widespread; some design research teams travel the world to do fieldwork locally themselves, supported by local translators and fixers who make all local arrangements, including finding participants. Analysis may be done on location, or 'at home' once all data is collected. Other design research teams stay at home and recruit remote data collectors, who get a detailed instruction for how to engage with participants, make notes and deliver initial, local insights. The design research lead then centrally analyses the data from all remote data collectors.

STBY and its Reach Network have developed a third approach, that combines some of these elements, and underpins the sensitivity to identifying what is meaningful to people in the context of their relation to particular organisations, products or services. For this purpose design researchers operate as close as possible to the local participants and their context, and are able to deeply understand these subtle signifiers. We put a strong emphasis on working with design researchers who are firmly grounded in the local context and culture. This ensures that local cultural, social, economic and historic contexts are deeply understood by the design researchers who do both data collection and analysis.

To ensure that such an international collaborative approach not only generates a collection of disconnected sets of local insights, it is of key importance that the local teams share their work on an ongoing basis. Together, they analyse and interpret the data sets, and draw out the overarching global insights and specific, meaningful local insights. To make this possible, all teams need to work according to a similar approach, with sufficient flexibility to localise the methods used. By working closely together with design researchers in other regions they can gather and analyse data across localities to identify meaningful commonalities and differences.

How to collaborate for a good balance between the local and the global, both during fieldwork and analysis, is an interesting challenge that we expect to spend a lot more energy on in the coming years. The interest for global design research is growing, driven by a market need but also by some excellent work that has been done. This requires all of us in this field to reflect on and further develop how we collaborate globally.

We do a lot of in-person 'syncs'. At least once per year we have a big event where we all meet and work together. This has a domino effect. You know the big team, you keep in touch with the smaller teams, and you work closely with some individuals. You do get better outcomes when you meet in person. Big organisations know and support that.
Katie Tzanidou

We are still a very centralised company. Most of our employees are here in New York. Yet many of our buildings and products are not. We are setting up teams there, and we give them capabilities, but research and design is not yet a part of that. It could be in the future, but not yet. We have a lot of growing up to do even before we go there. We have a lot of basic challenges before we address this one. Tomer Sharon

16

By its nature, innovation is not an efficient process. It's very specific to innovation that you need personal interaction, trust, and space to take risks. The thing about innovation is that you don't know the outcome. All of these aspects mean that you have to establish a very special human relationship. I work in a company that is all about communication, and we have all of the digital communication platforms to use. Although everything is at our fingertips, actually physically meeting is still so important, especially in a complex system like a large corporation. For me, working with purely virtual forms of communication is not sufficient when it comes to innovation. Andreas Sommerwerk

What I have seen in many organisations is that innovation is mostly happening at a very local level. Different departments will be working on the same issues sometimes without knowing it. Everyone at a more strategic level is aware that institutional learning is important, but not many organisations are good at it. I've seen in both private and non-profit organisations that the capability and methodologies used for this are either very weak or absent. When learning on a global level does take place in organisations, it tends to be very verbal, informal and managed by individuals. This makes it really difficult to replicate and scale. The institutionalization of these learnings, and how these things can be replicated, is something that we can still improve. Myrtille Danse

Collaboration on a global level has its challenges. For instance, we collaborate a lot with peers in distributed offices. The most obvious challenge is around time zones. How do you get over that without any of the parties not feeling respected? The needs of everyone should be taken into account. This is a big challenge. We have found that rotating times helps – so it is not always the same team who feels the pain of getting in early or staying up late. Katie Tzanidou

Andreas Sommerwerk is Service Design Manager at Deutsche Telekom AG. He is based in Berlin. He has a background in design, and previously worked for T-Mobile, Siemens and Panasonic in both Germany and Japan.

Katie Tzanidou is UX Research Manager at Google. She is based in London. Having previously worked for Paypal, she has extensive experience in working in dispersed research teams for global corporations.

Myrtille Danse is the Director of the Latin American Hub at Hivos, an international NGO that seeks new solutions to persistent global issues by facilitating social innovation. She is currently based in San Jose, Costa Rica. Myrtille has lived and worked across Europe, Africa, Asia and Latin America in various roles for companies, research institutes, NGOs and government.

Tomer Sharon is Head of UX at WeWork. Based in New York, he is responsible for their international design research. Tomer also also the author of the books 'Validating Product Ideas: Through Lean User Research' and 'It's Our Research: Getting Stakeholder Buy-in for User Experience Research Projects'.

Reframing global innovation

Digital technology has expanded the potential to collaborate across the globe enormously, and we probably have not seen the end of it yet. This supports global innovation massively, but it has not (yet) created a level playing field across the globe, as some suggest[1]. Innovation is still very much rooted in Western models, approaches and thought — mostly American and European. Even in Japan, with its strong culture of innovation, Western models are still common. Looking from a global perspective, it is clear to see that most patents are coming from these areas[2]. So how global is innovation, actually?

Innovative, creative organisations and people are all around the world; that is clear. We can see that through our Reach Network, and there are many, many more of course. However, these people and organisations are not equally supported by local business, financial, scientific, and educational networks in comparison to Western countries and Japan. Innovation policies and support are very unevenly distributed around the world, with most efforts visible in the West and Japan, and China catching up quickly. This tends to draw top global talent to the places where the best support is available, and leave other regions with bottom-up grassroots approaches, which have great value as well, but often struggle to achieve scale.

As a consequence, non-Western approaches, models, and thought on global innovation remain less prominent.

There must be potential for a more diverse perspective on and practice of innovation. This may be far away still, but we are keen to help innovation worldwide to develop in this more diverse direction where a level playing field exists not just on a technological but also economical, educational, scientific, and financial level. As a global design research community we will need to put more effort into developing non-Western perspectives on innovation, and in making these relevant and meaningful to the entire planet. Zooming out in space and time perhaps allows for a more realistic perspective of what could lie ahead. Emerging economies, especially in Asia, Africa and Latin America, will no doubt create a world that looks different from today's. We look forward to a future with more diverse global design research projects, partners, clients, and participants. We will all need to step out of some comfort zones and be prepared to 'make the strange familiar, and the familiar strange,'[3] but isn't that what global design research is about anyway? If we manage to do so as global design researchers, there is a great opportunity to reframe what global innovation can contribute to people's lives on this planet.

> Looking at technological innovation and spaces for social innovation, there are more opportunities in the West simply because many organisations tend to have bigger budgets and access to government funding. In most developing countries that just doesn't exist. You have to go to a bank and get a loan, which is risky. This creates a big difference. Government support decreases the risk level, because it makes funding available. If you look at it from this perspective, the global innovation playing field is not even at the moment. Myrtille Danse

> Large corporations tend to have their headquarters in one place, while a lot of the people work in distributed offices around the world. I see and respect that a lot of effort is spent in creating equal power and opportunities across distributed teams, but this is really very hard. The reality of working in distributed offices- the inherent imbalances- cannot be magically eliminated. This may need support for stronger leadership roles in the distributed offices, so they can also start building that scope — rather than just being a resource that tries to execute the ideas that are coming out of the headquarters. Katie Tzanidou

Innovation is an odd word to me. I take it in a very practical way. Actually, it is very straightforward and simple: innovation happens. You make an intentional effort and investment to learn about the needs of your audience that you were not aware of. Innovation happens when you make an effort to listen to what is working and what is not working. If something is not working, you have an innovation challenge to solve that — or people will just stop using your product. You must make an effort to find out why, and try to meet the needs you did not meet before. Tomer Sharonu

The environment for innovation is not level across the globe. Access to information in developing countries is not the same as in western countries for instance. This has its consequences for the speed of innovation. In some places, where the thinking around innovation is still new, people can be more guarded and even a bit selfish about it. Information is power, so if you have "the book" you are seen to be ahead. In places where this thinking is widely accepted, it's not about if you have the book. Everyone can get the book. It's more about how you put things into practice. Myrtille Danse

If you look at the DNA of the dominant thinking on innovation today, you can trace a lot back to the US or the West more generally. In many ways, I see our understanding of innovation as very democratic. We make an effort to involve many people in the process. In that sense it is very Western as well, stemming from the ideals of the enlightenment. Of course there is the mix and influence as things get shaken-up in the global innovation gene pool, but the core of the DNA is still coming from the West. This will take a long time to dilute. Andreas Sommerwerk

The global aspect of design research is clearly a key frontier for design research. This relates to how we understand people, as well as how we work, and how we view the world. We hope that the collection of stories, thoughts, cases, and illustrations in this publication will spark a conversation among our fellow researchers working for and within organisations grappling with the flattening of the world. We also hope to engage those working outside of design and research, to consider the benefits of embedding design research in strategising for their company or organisation. Enjoy the read, there is much to discuss!

1   Friedman, T. (2005). The World Is Flat. A Brief History of the Twenty-First Century. Farrar, Straus and Giroux.
2   Florida, R. (2005). The World is Spiky. *The Atlantic Monthly*, pp 48-51.
3   "The notion of 'making the familiar strange, and the strange familiar' is now a recurrent feature of artistic and photographic manifestos and of creative 'brainstorming' sessions in many fields. The phrase itself has been attributed to the German poet Novalis (1772-1801), aka Friedrich von Hardenberg." Quoted from: Chandler, D. (2001). *Semiotics: The Basics*. Routledge.

NETWORKS

Supporting global innovation

NETWORKS FOR NETWORKS

Supporting global innovation through design research means being able to respond to and cater for questions and calls for input on strategic dilemmas, coming from all parts of the organisation. Design researchers, whether they are working inside or outside client organisations, are supporting stakeholders in the organisation with making confident decisions about design, technology, marketing and communications. The requests for support can come from any team or department, and often the various stakeholders involved are working in different locations. It is not only the scope of global design research that is dispersed; the practice and delivery also are. Understanding this as a given has shaped our ways of collaborating and organising.

Networked modus operandi in client organisations
Global innovation efforts usually span explorations and experiments at different locations at the same time. This holds true for multi-national corporations as well as for international non-governmental organisations. Most likely the central HQ is involved — in setting direction, and in providing funding and training. At the same time, various local and national teams will be involved, as they are the ones who are likely to do the actual work in terms of delivering and implementing services, and they are also the ones who have the most contact with actual beneficiaries such as customers, citizens, patients, students, or employees. This means that most large scale organisations operate as 'networks', and global innovation needs to happen in the context of this modus operandi.

Networked collaboration and delivery by agencies
Global design research, as an integral part of global innovation, needs to cater for the networked modus operandi of large scale organisations. A good way to do this is to operate as a networked agency that is able to effectively connect to the various nodes in the client network. This has proven to be an approach that offers both the proximity needed for intense collaboration and local alignment, and the flexibility needed to engage people in the relevant regions for each project.

Networked audiences / target groups / beneficiaries
With the world being more connected, yet still unique in each part, it is only by creating deep empathy with people in their own everyday context that organisations can create solutions their customers love and that last in the changing global environment. Global design research is a useful approach to explore commonalities as well as differences between audiences and target groups around the world. As we all live in the same 21st century and on the same planet, we do have a lot in common. Even though not everyone may be able to use, or choose to use, the same technologies, products or services, most of us do know about them and in some way do still relate to them. Global design research aims to explore the balance between global shared insights and local specific insights.

The Reach Network for global design research

The Reach Network

The Reach Network was founded in 2008, in response to requests from clients who were interested in finding a better balance between their general global service offerings and bespoke offerings for specific local contexts. The partners in the network are relatively small, agile and independent businesses with a deep expertise in design research.

All the partners are seasoned professionals who are firmly grounded in their local culture. This facilitates faster, cheaper, and more effective international collaborations than those possible via traditional models, which often rely on local translators, freelancers and local assistants supporting lead researchers who visit multiple global locations in order to ensure consistency.

The Reach Network undertakes international projects at scale while maintaining the agility and flexibility of small, independent design companies embedded in a local context. The strong collaboration between the international partners in the Reach Network drives design research at a local level while maintaining a global vision. This has helped clients deepen their understanding of customers in multiple markets without having to reach out to individual expertise in each location.

The highly experienced teams of designers and researchers in the Reach Network seamlessly integrate design research activities in wider innovation processes, offering client teams an empathic sparring partner by highlighting the voice of the customer throughout the various stages.

The Reach Network currently has 12 partners, located in 15 countries around the world. New partners are joining the network in response to relevant activities happening in other parts of the world. Currently a few new partners in Africa and South East Asia are about to join. See the website for the most up-to-date information: www.globaldesignresearch.com

For each project, a relevant selection of partners is involved. A strong shared perspective and trust is key to this collaboration. Between the partners exists a generous culture of sharing ideas, experiences and materials. Over the years we have built up and nurtured an open and flexible style of collaboration, and this has proven to be very effective. It ensures that each experienced design research team can contribute to the maximum of their abilities without being micro-managed. It goes without saying that on a more formal level the network also has all the necessary paperwork between the partners in place, such as mutual non-disclosure agreements, project contracts, project administration, secure shared online server space and a set of online

collaboration tools. Being experienced professionals working for large-scale corporate clients, these things are part and parcel of normal daily routines. The Reach Network allows partners to handle large scale and complex international design research projects, without compromising on being agile, flexible and sensitive to local nuances.

To ensure a consistent level of quality, and a minimum level of stress for the client teams, the Reach Network adheres to effective project management. One of the partners involved usually acts as the primary contractor for a client. Most often this is the partner that is closest to where the client is based. The primary contractor will make sure that all participating partners from the network deliver fully, on time and within budget, and provide a guarantee of quality of all services and deliverables.

For instance, if a project starts in London, then STBY is usually the main contractor, and the other partners from the network are sub-contracted. However, these partners are quite independent in the way they conduct their local fieldwork and the analysis. The strong shared methodology for Reach projects allows for centrally prepared materials to be used locally in slightly different ways to suit the local context. Most important is to make sure that all the teams work with the same focus and structure the data in a way that makes it easy to synthesise during analysis and delivery. Clients often want results fast and for a limited budget, so all the partners involved are keen to not waste time on endless discussions or endless experiments. The ongoing work is frequently aligned via shared online workspaces and frequent video conferences. We also have procedures and tools to support remote collaboration, such as weekly status calls, milestones reporting, shared calendaring and SSL-secured online file repositories.

Being true pioneers of global design research, all partners in Reach are keen to share and further develop their own knowledge. Not just amongst each other, but also with the wider community of peers in the field. Our Great Outdoors Of Design conferences (a.k.a. GOOD) have attracted attention from a wide range of peers and experts from all over the world. We have hosted two of these international conferences together. The first one was in 2011 in London, and the second one in 2013 in Eindhoven.

Several Reach partners also host their own annual conferences like UXHK (by Apogee in Hong Kong) and Unbox (by Quicksand in New Delhi). During the UXHK conference in 2015 the Reach Network also moderated a seminar on global design research.

Thoughts on Global Design Research from the Reach Network

Reach Network members pride themselves on being reflective practitioners. In line with this, many agencies in the network publish regularly in various different formats, and present at different events and conferences. These sections present handpicked content and photos that nicely illustrate some thoughts about global design research from our partners around the world.

APOGEE

Jo Wong and Dan Szuc are partners at Apogee, based in Hong Kong. Apogee's primary focus is to help businesses gain a deeper understanding of the outside world, by shifting their view from inward and company-centric to empathic and customer-focused - to help people "Make Meaningful Work". Apogee have a strong track record of doing design research across mainland China. They are also a strong force in strengthening human-centred design in Asia. Since 2011 they annually organise the UX Hong Kong conference, which brings together all product and service design disciplines - from research to marketing, design, technology and business - who are interested and passionate about designing great experiences for people and business for a better world for all.

"When we started pitching the importance of related disciplines like usability and user centered design 10+ years ago in Hong Kong and in mainland China, there was little interest or understanding of what the terms meant, how they could be applied in product design and development, or how it could help the business make better products and services. Fast forward to today, and we are seeing encouraging trends and indicators in the Asian market to show that User Experience is healthy, growing and will continue to do well for many years to come."[1]

"As businesses in Asia in various domains look to how they can mature, differentiate and compete globally in their respective products and services, User Experience (UX) is gaining significant momentum. Management are curious as to what UX means and how it can be applied to not just improve experiences but to create real delight. They are looking for people and professional communities to support them in this change. This is being helped by Asian companies investing in design, and there has been an increase in design studios and research and development offices opening up locally. Also companies from outside Asia

want to get a deeper understanding of the Asian mindsets and cultures—especially in growth markets like mainland China—so they can design more effectively for their needs and preferences."[2]

"It is important to recognize and celebrate diversity. But we should also ensure that we don't focus too much on our differences for the sake of their being differences, rather than understanding how our differences and similarities play out in the designs we create and the work that we do. We must be able to appreciate where we all come from and give that the respect it deserves, but, at the same time, let ourselves move toward being able to see new moments and opportunities."[3]

"Bring back more than just facts and snapshots. Think about the real lives behind your observations. What are people's personal narratives? How are they related to your own experience, viewpoints, or ways of thinking? When you bring back your experiences in other cultures to share with your colleagues, tell the underlying story with empathy."[4]

1   Szuc, D., Wong, J. (2012). The Landscape of User Experience
     Design in Asia. Core77 [digital source]. Retrieved from:
     http://www.core77.com/posts/21474/the-landscape-of-user-
     experience-design-in-asia-by-daniel-szuc-and-josephine-
     wong-21474
2   Ibid.
3   Queensbury, W., Szuc, D. (2012). Global UX: A Journey.
     UX Matters [digital source]. Retrieved from: http://www.uxmatters.
     com/mt/archives/2012/01/global-ux-a-journey.php
4   Ibid.

MATCHBOXOLOGY

Jason Coetzee and Cal Bruns are two of the partners at Matchboxology, a 'Design For Impact' consultancy based in Johannesburg and Cape Town, South Africa. They help leaders and organisations change behaviors and systems to improve lives. Matchboxology has been developing African based human-centred design expertise for over a decade and this remains the guiding principle in their work. They are frequently on assignment for public and private sector projects across the continent.

Jason: Matchboxology works across the African continent, with global NGOs and brands. What approach have you found that works well across all these situations where change and innovation are needed?

Cal: The team at Matchboxology have over a decade's experience working with leaders in the private and public sectors across nine countries on our continent. While 'human-centred design' (HCD) is most commonly applied to designing products and software, we've been pioneering its use in a variety of behaviour-change contexts. Being based in Africa has given us the opportunity to be especially relevant to a variety of prevention programmes in public health. Here we've seen HCD consistently give us the lens with which to gain a deeper empathy for risky behaviours.

Public health programmes are guided by extensive evidence from qualitative and quantitative research. Teams of international experts funded by large donor nations and private foundations focus on supporting under-resourced governments with global best practice advice and programmes. But we consistently see significant gaps in what experts have determined populations of people should do, and what those populations of people want to do. HCD has become a new and valuable tool for international development

because it adds a significant new member to the problem-solving team: ordinary people.

Jason: So how do you involve ordinary people in your pan-African approach?

Cal: We do HCD immersion sessions that take us into our subject's world, where we field direct conversations as opposed to conduct interviews. While existing qualitative and quantitative research fills known knowledge gaps, we've found our sessions help to discover highly valuable information that we didn't know we didn't know. We're observing with our ears and our eyes for those perceptions, attitudes and barriers (both physical and social) that drive the way people currently behave. At Matchboxology, we've learned the value of conducting immersion sessions across the full ecosystem—from funders to experts to local implementing and government partners as well as the target audience and their community. This wider net gives a more accurate picture of all the dynamics impacting a particular challenge.

We've found fielding immersion sessions is an art. One not only needs to be a keen and objective observer and skilled interviewer, but has to have that rare ability to instantly gain a subject's trust. We've seen time and time again; trust generates truth. Once we're armed with a deep empathy for the full ecosystem's beliefs, behaviours and motivators, we have a far better ability to accurately frame specific challenges leading to positive social impact.

Jason: Once you've gained this empathy and deep understanding of the entire ecosystem, what do you do with that?

Cal: We then move into a second valuable element HCD adds to the development toolkit; collective problem-solving and prototyping. While the traditional path to solutions is to feed qualitative and quantitative evidence and data to experts who then produce a solution, Matchboxology's HCD methodology curates a collective problem-solving team made up of experts and folks from the full

ecosystem. We use our immersion session phase to help us recruit excellent candidates for this collective.

Let me give you an example that illustrates how this collective problem-solving can be very successful if everyone is collaborating as absolute equals. A funny thing happened while standing on a very rickety chair, facilitating a HCD session in rural Sierra Leone. I discovered that HCD has the ability to change the entire future of Africa.

My audience was a group of community health workers, nurses, Ministry of Health officials, teachers, villagers and chiefs, local NGO employees and global experts. Standing on that chair, I was demonstrating to them how difficult it is for people to communicate and collaborate when one person looms above others based on rank, authority or perceived superiority.

I invited a villager to stand on his chair and face me. I promise you we were both very uncomfortable teetering on those wobbling chairs in that hot workshop room and everyone in the audience was concerned for our safety! I made my point that when everyone is equally uncomfortable in a fun situation, we are indeed equals and the creativity can really flow. A hand went up and what this local district councilman said next rocked my world.

"I'm sorry to interrupt, but if we use this thinking, we could have a very peaceful society and world. This is not a brainstorming technique, this is a skill to make us a better country. This equality and empathy is powerful. Don't you think your HCD could solve all our problems if we could teach every citizen to apply it?"

We've fielded HCD to positively change development programmes, organisations and product design. We've applied it to create measurable positive behaviour change in public health. And to generate better government policies. I'd never thought about it, but the man has a point. Here's to hoping some enlightened African leader will take the next step and deploy HCD to create happier communities and a better country that inspires a true African renaissance. If you're a president and reading this, please give me a call!

QUICKSAND

Ayush Chauhan and Babitha George are partners at Quicksand, an interdisciplinary consultancy in Delhi, Bangalore and Goa. Quicksand is globally recognized for its expertise in user-centred innovation for emerging markets. Their work supports organisations in envisioning programs, products and services that are future facing, disruptive, and yet rooted in principles of human-centred design.

Ayush: Can you trace, through some examples perhaps, how the studio's understanding of human-centred design has changed over the years?

Babitha: At some level, I think it was a basic curiosity and our love for stories and travel that spurred our foray into human-centred design, which is at its core about empathy and deep understanding of people's needs and designing for those needs. A lot of our projects have taken us to interesting places where we have had the chance to delve into myriad contexts. Whether it was looking at designing a phone helpline system for education, where we went to rural West Bengal and spent time with government school teachers, or more recently, attempting to address the plastic bag challenge in Cambodia, most of our projects have taken us to spaces where we have had a chance to embed ourselves deeply within

a context and listen and observe— with humility, openness and a learning attitude. In that sense, it feels like we worked through our own process of human-centred design and constantly adapted in order to make meaning for all our stakeholders. Probably it was liberating to not tie ourselves down in buzz words and definitions.

A lot of our projects have also thrown us into unfamiliar contexts, within India but also across Asia and Africa. However, our primary need to stay true to real people's needs and aspirations, ensured that we went in with curiosity —while simultaneously building on the practice and learnings that we evolved over the years— and built local partnerships (as we were cognizant of the fact that deep contextual understanding cannot be built instantaneously). And this approach has constantly held us in good stead across contexts.

Ayush: Can you speak about how this idea of human-centred design permeates the studio practice outside of just the methodology that we would apply on various projects?

Babitha: The idea of making sense of our attempts in a highly personal manner, whether in client projects or independent pursuits, has ensured that we stay true to the core idea of human-centred design even within the studio. The way the studio practice has evolved over the years has not been through an impersonal fashion, but in a manner that took into account all of our collective interests and aspirations. This

passion to ground all of our efforts in honest enquiry and understanding what people really want to experience, has permeated not just client projects, but also independent pursuits such as UnBox.

Whether it is about the studio rallying around personal interests and motivations or about creating communities of practice with external partners and friends, there is always a humane basis to our pursuits, irrespective of the scale. How can we create an engaging festival experience, if we did not involve partners in the co-creation of it? How can we build rich learning experiences, without allowing for flexibility in that journey, to account for what participants can bring to it? How can we engage with a range of external experts on independent, bootstrapped ventures, if we cannot relate first as friends and partners?

The nature of our work may change over the coming years, but I hope that the soul of it does not and we continue to build on these ideas of curiosity, honesty, and empathy with an extended community of partners and friends.

Find the full-length interview on Quicksand's Medium page: https://medium.com/hello-qs/a-conversation-on-human-centered-design-bf2e338e0e26

> "
> AS A TRANS-DISCIPLINARY PRACTICE, QUICKSAND'S POSITION OF STRENGTH LIES AT THE CONFLUENCE OF DISCIPLINES LIKE DESIGN, BUSINESS, ARTS, SOCIAL SCIENCE AND TECHNOLOGY.

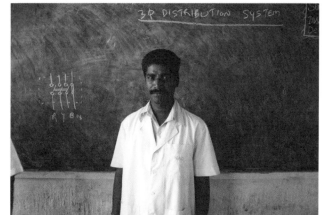

FUELFOR

Fuelfor designs healthcare experiences that work for people. They have built a deep expertise in the healthcare domain over the last 18 years, with a strong capability and track record in insights-based design and strategy. They are based in Barcelona and Singapore. The Care Lab is an associated initiative, launching soon. Stay tuned here: https://www.thecarelab.org

These film stills are from a 'behind-the-scenes' video summarising fuelfor's extensive caregiving project for Singapore's National Council of Social Service (NCSS). Although not a global project in and of itself, the researchers,

clients and participants all represent culturally diverse backgrounds. This project nicely illustrates how, at the end of the day, we are all human and how ethnography can elicit empathy and a shared vision within an organisation. The methods used throughout the research also demonstrate the power of visual design research in developing a rich understanding of human context, clearly distinguishing it from other forms of research. The full video can be viewed online at http://www.fuelfor.net/caregiving.

"In this project we went to people's homes, entered their lives, followed them along their journeys, cried with them, laughed with them, they shared with us the things that they treasured... and then we took all of these back

to inform the premise of concepts to hopefully create a better experience in the next few years for our clients." **Yeok Nguan, Senior Assistant Director, NCSS**

"Before the research started my initial impression of caregiving was that it was tough, but I didn't know how tough. I also didn't really know how beautiful it can also be. The caregivers showed me what pure love is." **Annet Bruil, Design Researcher, fuelfor**

"The biggest tool in this project is film. It allows us to get a certain level of intimacy but also provides this visual information that really uncovers the whole context and experience in such a sensorial way." **Lekshmy Parameswaran, Co-founder, fuelfor**

CASE STUDY #1
Multi-stage international design research, exploring new strategic concept directions

This case study describes a design research project commissioned by a major global technology company. The company was keen to explore whether a new concept direction they were considering developing would meet the needs and interest of several target groups in three global locations, and specifically wanted to know which aspects of this concept would best match with the everyday lives of these consumers. The international design research involved empathic interactions with over 120 participants in the UK, Spain, and Russia, producing strategic insights on their preferences, motivations and expectations. These insights were visually supported by short films containing individual participant stories, and presented to a large number of internal stakeholders. The research team for this project consisted of STBY, who coordinated the research whilst also conducting the fieldwork in the UK section, and two Reach partners, Summ()n and fuelfor, who conducted the fieldwork in Russia and Spain respectively and actively contributed to the final analysis and delivery.

Defining the focus, methodology and process

As this project had two distinct goals, we had to think carefully about which methodology to adopt. Firstly, an innovative concept direction had to be introduced to several different groups of consumers in order to elicit their feedback on its purpose, design, functionality and intended context of use. Since the input material consisted of a non-functioning first model, a range of creative exercises had to be developed that would allow participants to explore the 'mental model' of the concept to the required level of detail. As the project also sought to explore the specific local contexts of use around the new concept, this required a markedly different approach, which focused on gathering data in relation to people's local behaviours, routines, aspirations and apprehensions to allow for the concept to be further fleshed out later.

The chosen methodology entailed a multi-stage approach, in which an initial series of User Experience Labs (see below) held across three global locations enabled the team to do a 'wide splash' of explorations with 120 different participants. Several people were then selected from this large group for individual 'deep dive' ethnographic immersions in context. These were more detailed, and focused on their motivations, behaviours, aspirations and apprehensions concerning the technology involved. This second methodology we call Design Documentaries (see below).

From the outset, the project was meant to maintain both a global and a local focus. Both of the research goals detailed above were to be examined in three different locations by three different teams, with the possibility to analyse the data jointly towards both global and local insights into the cultural influences at play. For this to be feasible, you need to have a joint process across locations and local teams that is flexible enough to be adjusted to local situations, needs, etiquette and even ethics. You need to maintain a balance between global and local, and that is what the process we followed was designed to facilitate.

Recruitment and selection

At the start, the client provided a range of characteristics for the different groups they would like to get feedback from. We worked with them to refine the recruitment profiles in relation to the project's goal, in order to ensure that the aims for the research could be met. Once this had been agreed, we completed a detailed set of participant specifications that local teams then aligned with their local recruitment agencies, making local adjustments where needed to achieve the globally agreed profiles. Regular contact between all parties involved was vital throughout this process to ensure that the emerging samples could be fine-tuned before participants were finalised. Thorough documentation of this process meant the recruiting could be aligned along similar lines in all research locations, achieving a consistency in the global sample which was crucial for the subsequent analysis.

Local cultural factors which might skew a research profile were also taken into account. This required close collaboration between the local partners – each an expert in their region's culture. Recruitment, just like research, cannot simply be 'cut and pasted' from one location to the next. Ultimately a complex sample based around a variety of demographic and socio-economic variables was recruited both on time and on budget.

Research guidelines as common point of reference

The research guide provided all the local teams with specifications on how the aims of the project were to be met within the timeframe and budget available. Rather than developing a research plan with an overly prescriptive set of 'rules' which aren't flexible enough to be useful as a project evolves, Reach's preferred approach to this is to produce a set of 'Research Guidelines'. These guidelines cover each step in the proposed process, outlining both the activities to be undertaken and the intended outputs of each of these stages, while providing enough flexibility to adjust for local specifics. The guidelines act as a common point of reference for both the research teams and the client team, ensure a consistency of approach across locations,

and provide a clear indication of the various research materials which need to be developed as well as the outputs that are expected.

Research materials for effective data collection and documentation

The principle of general guidelines rather than rules extended to the research materials that supported the engagements with the participants, who had to be probed on their behaviours, needs, and motivations in a manner which would provoke insightful, engaging and accurate responses. With the effective use of research materials, the participants in all three locations completed individual exercises, worked in small groups to build and construct models, and even developed their own imagined solutions which they were asked to present on video.

These research materials elicited structured local results which could be quickly and easily interpreted during a joint collaborative workshop with the full design research team. This structured the data set enabled the local teams to identify emerging local insights using a common 'language' that would form the basis of the joint analysis.

User Experience Labs

Several different types of consumers were invited to join the User Experience Labs, our first methodology, in which their behaviours, routines, and perceptions could be explored and recorded. The purpose of these workshop sessions was to learn about the experiences of the participant with products, services and situations similar to the concept ideas. The goal was to make these sessions as engaging and interactive as possible. A series of unique exercises were carefully designed to elicit thoughtful responses, grounded in people's own experiences whilst also provoking speculations about how the new concept (of which we had early prototypes on hand during the sessions) would fit in the the participants' lives.

Moderated by the local research teams, the sessions facilitated an open, collaborative, and focused exploration of the topic, in a way that could be consistently replicated

across the locations involved. The emphasis placed on engagement also extended to the client team. Drawn from a predominantly marketing background, they were used to observing such sessions from behind a screen, whereas Reach's approach instead encourages more involvement in the sessions, and direct contact with the participants. The client team also invited colleagues from their local offices to attend the user labs so they could directly benefit from the interactions with the participants.

Design Documentaries

A subsequent round of ethnographic immersions in the real-live contexts of the individual participants in all three cities allowed the local research teams to explore some of the findings from the User Experience Labs in even more detail. The group sessions allowed the teams to identify the most relevant candidates for the immersions, and to get an idea about the best stories to further explore in the follow-up immersion.

To capture these stories in context, we used the Design Documentaries methodology, which resulted in a repository of some 60 short films, each containing one story from one participant (also see the next chapter on Practice for a more detailed description of this methodology). Together these films examined the project topic in a number of real-world contexts and from several perspectives in different locations. In this way, the immersions added another level of detail that could only be derived from speaking with people at length in the environments where they typically perform and experience the activities we were interested in.

review and pre-analysis

On completion of the fieldwork, the local Reach partners collaborated on a joint review of all the data gathered. This pre-analysis resulted in a shortlist of the stories that were most relevant to draw out from the immersions and craft into visually illustrated narratives to share with the client stakeholders. The labs and immersions generated a great deal of material, which could be interpreted in a number of ways and used to tell a variety of stories. Prioritisation is crucial, and when done in close collaboration with the client team, offers an excellent opportunity for them to get

an early understanding of the emerging local and global insights, while allowing them to make sure the final results are focused on the organisation's objectives.

Synthesised analysis and report

The final analysis for this project was undertaken in a collaborative workshop that brought together the three local research teams and the core client team. In this workshop, the results of both the User Experience Labs and the Design Documentaries were synthesised and refined into a final set of the most interesting and relevant insights and opportunities.

Interpreting data from people with diverse local backgrounds, with several different voices and perspectives, is an inevitable part of collaborative analysis, even more so in global design research. Structuring our discussions around the evidence (structured materials from the workshops and the short films) helped to anchor the analysis in real-world examples, and to keep the conversations focused. The benefit of placing such an emphasis on output within this collaborative context is

the greatly enhanced ownership participants feel over the results, and the ease with which these results can then be communicated to a wider audience in the client organisation.

The workshop was also designed around the diverse stakeholders who participated. The core client team wanted to use the workshop to introduce a number of colleagues from various departments (e.g. marketing, strategy, design) to the research, and involve them in the analysis. The presence of the research teams of each of the three locations enhanced the local cultural perspectives in the research material that had been collected.

Visualisation and presentation of opportunity areas

The results of the workshop were then processed into a poster that provided a visual summary of the identified opportunity areas in an easily accessible way. This 'at a glance' introduction to the initial results proved to be highly useful when communicating the results within the client organisation, and in particular to the teams that had

to work with the results in detail. The joint research team also developed a detailed debrief presentation and report, and delivered these to a high number of stakeholders in an extensive worldwide conference call. This introduced a large audience to the existence of the work, and the evidence base underpinning it – in particular, the films that helped to raise empathy within the teams.

Making sure the final delivery was successful and relevant to all stakeholders required close collaboration with the client team. The presentation we designed went through several iterations to make sure it related to strategic priorities, and the provision of video to an internal audience in six global locations required careful logistical preparation. A compilation film was made out of a selection of the short films, to be used in executive meetings high up in the organisation, effectively encapsulating the headline findings while retaining some of the underlying evidence.

Value for the client organisation
The documentation of the User Experience Labs provided a summary of the feedback on the initial concept that could be cross-referenced against both consumer profiles and locations. This feedback covered the purpose, style, and

functionality of the prototypes that had been introduced, with some findings particular to specific locations and others relevant in a wider global context.

Mapping the opportunity areas and detailing these with further concept directions provided a cohesive overview of how the original concept related to people's lives. The feedback from the User Experience Labs was thus anchored into a structured account of people's everyday lives, adding a behavioural component to the overall concept being reviewed.

The Design Documentaries produced from the immersions were used to identify and explore a number of further potential opportunity areas in relation to the initial concept. In the joint workshop these were developed into a series of new additional concept directions. Several of these concept directions appeared to be relevant across the locations covered by the research, while others were more specific to particular local circumstances and environments.

Ultimately the client team came out of the project with a much clearer view of how consumers in the various markets would respond, what attributes it would need to succeed, what changes might need to be made, and what additional concept directions could be relevant.

CASE STUDY #2
International co-development and prototyping of the DIY Toolkit

Co-funded by Nesta and The Rockefeller Foundation, the Reach partners STBY (UK) and Quicksand (India) together developed the DIY Toolkit in a staged process of iterative prototyping, testing, and refinement. In this project the global design research was an integral part of the development process of the toolkit.

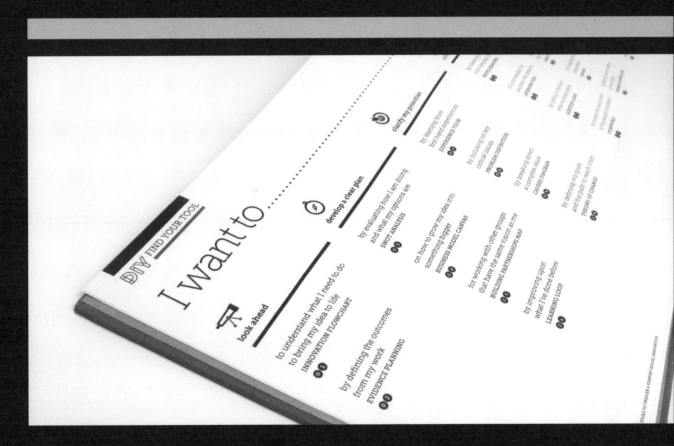

The full name of the toolkit is: 'Development Impact and You: Practical Tools for Social Innovation'. From the outset the toolkit was primarily meant for practitioners in international development, but since its launch in 2014 it has been a breakthrough success in many different sectors, including design, business, education and policy development.

The toolkit contains a set of 30 best-in-class and proven tools that aim to trigger and support social innovation. Every tool has a concise description, a downloadable worksheet, some practical instructions and a tutorial video with examples that show how the tools can be used. Many

The DIY toolkit book, available to download at diytoolkit.org

tools also have one or more case studies that describe their use in the context of specific projects, organisations and cultures. The toolkit is published under a Creative Commons license and is therefore freely available online. On the website of the DIY Toolkit (diytoolkit.org) users can also share comments and rank the tools according to their experiences.

This project built on the results of an initial comprehensive landscape study conducted by Nesta, which found that while many effective tools were available, there was still a big gap when it came to tools being used in international development work. Many of these practitioners did not identify with 'innovation' or 'design' and therefore did not make use of the tools available from those fields. At the same time, they did express a clear need for a trusted and proven set of essential tools that are not only effective, but that can also inspire and practically support them at each relevant stage in their innovation journey, and in different contexts around the world. In particular, the Global South was mentioned frequently. Triggered by this challenge, STBY and Quicksand worked with Nesta to create a toolkit that is very human-centred, solution-driven, and collaborative in its approach; i.e. curated from the perspective of the practitioners. Contextualised with case studies and guidelines for usage, the tools give them the flexibility to adapt and apply these to a range of contexts. The toolkit enables these busy practitioners to find the right tools at the right moment for them.

"

THE EVIDENCE PLANNING TOOL HELPED US TO IDENTIFY TRIGGERS FOR ENSURING ENGAGEMENT WITH DIFFERENT COMMUNITY MEMBERS, AND IT EMPHASISED THE NEED FOR A WELL DESIGNED PROCESS FOR ENGAGEMENT. UNDP, Kosovo

Developing tools for social impact that aim to support and increase the innovation capacity of international development practitioners.

The iterative development of the toolkit was divided in three key phases, with the toolkit becoming more and more concrete as it evolved through each phase. Each stage had its own challenges, but spreading the core editorial and design work between STBY and Quicksand in two locations (London and New Delhi) was not one of them. Having worked together on many complex projects before, both teams were able to confidently collaborate. The use of online platforms for transparent sharing of work-in-progress, and frequent personal check-ins for alignment, enabled them to synchronise tasks and re-focus agendas from week to week.

The total development of the toolkit spanned a period of about seven months. Keen to produce a first prototype ready for testing with the international target group, we set ourselves the goal to complete the initial co-design and editing stage in only two months. The main challenge in this stage was to prioritise a shortlist of 30 tools from the vast repository of 200 tools that Nesta had already collected in the run-up to the project. An extensive joint review and selection process resulted in a set of tools that effectively represented the various stages of a social innovation process. In this process we made sure to not over-represent tools for user research and idea generation. In line with the Innovation Spiral from Nesta, we emphasised the inclusion of sufficient models and methods around strategic evidence

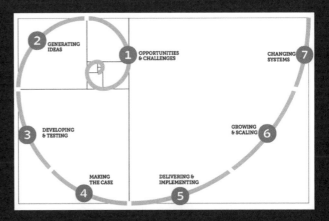

The Innovation Spiral by Nesta, describes the seven stages of the complex journey of innovation. It highlights an iterative approach rather than a linear one to allow for unpredictability and change.

> "
> THE TOOLS HELPED TO FAMILIARISE OURSELVES WITH THE LOCAL PROBLEM AND ROOT OUT ACTIONABLE CAUSES, SOME OF WHICH WERE UNEXPECTED AND NEW TO US. **UNDP, Uzbekistan**

planning and scalability. The input material for the selected 'tools' differed widely in shape and form. Even though all of them were proven and tested in their field, many of the tools from the business world were only documented as a textual description in a paper or book. Very few of them were 'toolkit-ready', as they lacked practical instructions or worksheets. At the same time, many of the tools from the design world were strongly visual, but often skewed towards branding and visual design. We realised that this might be the reason why so many practitioners in international development were not taking up the use of these tools. They needed more practical guidance and fewer glossy materials. This made us determined to focus on making accessible and easy-to-use worksheets for each tool, and to stay away from anything that needed full colour printing. With these guidelines, we edited and designed the selection of tools into a first prototype for the toolkit. During this period STBY and Quicksand were in constant direct contact with each other, as well as with the client team from Nesta and Rockefeller, in an open yet structured agile collaboration.

In the second phase of the iterative development project, the prototype of the toolkit was tested via a bespoke online platform by practitioners and organisations from various fields (education, health, financial inclusion, microfinance, rights & advocacy etc.) based in locations across the Global South (Asia, Africa, Latin America). The participants in the prototype test were invited through the extensive networks of the main partners in the project (Nesta, Rockefeller Foundation, STBY, Quicksand, and other Reach partners). To keep the main objective for the toolkit

at top of mind, we were careful to only include participants in the prototype test who were actual practitioners in international development. This meant we had to disappoint many other people who had heard about the project and were interested in trying the tools out. It was great to see how quickly a wide variety of people and organisations signed up to test out the tools in their everyday work, and how they provided us with considered feedback from their practical experience. To give the participants sufficient time for a serious test-drive of the tools at a relevant moment in their projects and work, we planned this second stage of the project to last for two months. An extra benefit of the feedback we collected on the use of the tools was that we gathered useful input for case studies in the slipstream of the prototype test that could be added to the toolkit as examples of use in various local contexts.

> "
> IN THE CAMBODIAN CONTEXT, ASKING A QUESTION WILL MOST LIKELY NOT GET YOU THE ANSWER RIGHT AWAY. RATHER, YOU HAVE TO ASK THE SAME QUESTION IN SEVERAL DIFFERENT WAYS. UNDERSTANDING WHICH QUESTIONS ARE MOST COMPLEX HELPED TO REMIND US TO ASK QUESTIONS AS SIMPLY AS POSSIBLE FIRST. **IDE, Cambodia**

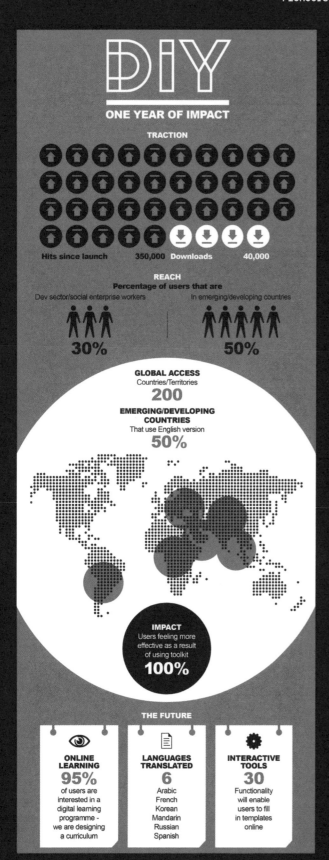

IT HELPED THE TEAM TO UNDERSTAND
THAT EVEN THEIR ROLES AS GRASSROOTS
WORKERS CAN CONTRIBUTE TO A LARGER
CHANGE OVER TIME. **MPTAST, India**

The teams who tried out the DIY Toolkit reported that it helped them to do their own local design research and use that to strengthen the overall operation and direction of their organisations, which were often global NGOs. The flexibility of the prototype tool designs was tested to the limit, in contexts with very limited printing possibilities, or lack of paper. Blackboards and whiteboards were used to recreate the tools, and some were even drawn in sand. This emphasised the need to keep tools simple enough to print them on basic black and white printers, possibly in parts no larger than A4 sizes, and even simple enough to use them without printing at all.

Based on the responses from the prototype test, the final version of the toolkit was then developed and finally launched in February 2014. This last stage took another three months, as the final iteration to the design and editing had to be done, as well as the full production of the website and the printed publication. The direct engagement with a wide network of practitioners during the development phase of the toolkit also proved to be an important accelerator for the interest in and uptake of the tools by individuals and organisations within the field. By the time the toolkit was launched, many organisations working in international development had in some way or another been engaged in the overall process, and were happy to endorse the outcomes. At the launch the toolkit was supported by global organisations such as UNDP, ICSF, OXFAM, SIX, Ushahidi, SiG, Innoweave, and ProjectInnovation. Many of these organisations now use the DIY Toolkit as training material in bootcamps and masterclasses. The decision by Nesta and the Rockefeller Foundation to provide the tools as open source materials has definitely been elemental in this. Judging from the feedback we have received since 2014, we can also conclude that our strong push for providing accessible worksheets for each tool and coming up with an easy to use navigational model (based on 'I want to....') has helped to trigger its success, as this is what makes the DIY Toolkit stand out from other existing toolkits in the field. By positioning global design research firmly in the middle of this creation process, we were able to carefully design the success of the tools rather than speculating what would be successful around the globe.

Global Training and Coaching

Capacity building in client organisations

In the process of collaborating on global innovation projects for clients, the partners in the Reach Network have accumulated a vast body of knowledge on how to conduct design research in several countries, either simultaneously or in phases. So beyond being asked to work on projects with clients and partners, we are also asked more and more to help with capacity building for service innovation in organisations. For these activities, we draw on our practice and expertise from the projects on the ground, as well as our deep understanding of the models and toolkits that are available to support them. We have developed some of those toolkits ourselves, but whenever relevant we also make use of other successful tools and methods. The client organisations that ask for capacity building are from both the corporate and the public or non-profit sector.

The REACH School

The Reach School was established to help organisations who want to build their internal design capacity for a global audience. A few partners in the Reach Network (STBY, Quicksand and Apogee) have piloted and co-developed this approach over the past few years in various locations and with a wide range of organisations. Its focus on capacity building for human-centred innovation and a co-creative approach to blended learning (combining offline and online teaching) make it stand out from traditional courses focusing on a more top-down transfer of knowledge. The partners in The Reach School share a belief that training should move beyond introducing toolkits and delivering one-off innovation courses. Based on years of experience working with clients from all sectors and sizes, the holistic training programme is comprised of three elements:

People
Proximity to the people who will be using and delivering the innovation is key to human-centred design. People should be ever-present throughout any innovation process.

Process
Process lays the foundation for continuous improvement. Tools and process provide structure to the typically fluid activity of human-centred design. Adjusting and adapting process to context is key to innovation practice.

Practice
Accumulating experience with design-driven innovation in different contexts builds a craft. With practice, people and process come together into a meaningful whole.

This three-level conceptual framework enables the participants in the training programme to better understand how effective global innovation happens and where their own practice fits in. Participants learn how to identify, interpret and work with meaningful cultural differences in the information provided from various sources, including marketers, ethnographers and others. They are guided through a number of intensive bespoke exercises in which they apply the tools to their existing design work, together with their colleagues.

The Reach School leverages the collective expertise and experience of the partners in the Reach Network. The major obstructions to innovation are effectively addressed through four delivery principles. We guide the learners in their practices, to help them develop the fluency of process required for successful innovation. Secondly, we illustrate the need and potential for process versatility through case studies of successful projects, to boost the learners' creative confidence in adapting their use of the tools and methods for specific contexts. We connect learners to local practitioners who are embedded in the wider global Reach Network, to support the replicability and scaling up of context-sensitive innovation. And finally, we coach and support learners, to make sure both their understanding and work practices are fundamentally changed through the training.

An initial series of interviews with the people involved in global innovation within the organisation establishes the challenges the organisation faces and the degree and kind of global and local knowledge their teams possess. The existing channels of learning, attitudes toward global design, and the existing global design process are also examined. This culminates in a report on the current practice in global innovation in the organisation, and lays the groundwork for the upcoming training sessions. A set of tools is then created specifically for the organisation and its markets, in the form of precise yet practically oriented documents, which the various teams (design, strategy and others) use to structure their internal conversations about meaningful differences that direct their work. The impact of the training is measured with an evaluation closely aligned to the concrete goals that have been established in advance. The evaluation includes visualisations of the most important feedback from participants.

Global design programme for multi-national corporations

For multinational companies with customers in various different cultures and locations, figuring out what matters in each, and what may create positive or negative responses, is no simple matter. The Reach School offers a structured approach that enables companies to successfully engage local markets on a global scale. We teach the design teams, product owners and others involved how to apply the approach and implement an effective and sustainable global design process.

EXAMPLE
Global UX Design training for a global online retailer

Millions of people in more than a hundred countries use the sites and applications of this company every day, in more than 20 languages. These visitors and customers represent a diversity of cultures. Knowing precisely how to tailor the user experience for them is critical to the success of the company.

This is no simple matter. The choices sellers and buyers make during a customer journey to take the next step, to trust a proposition or not, or to continue or break off a transaction, happen within a split second and are often motivated by minute design features that these website visitors are not consciously aware of. Figuring out which features those are, and which cultural differences cause which positive or negative responses, is difficult enough already, but applying this knowledge in the day-to-day design of the client's digital channels is even harder.

In collaboration with the company's Design Research and Strategy team, STBY (London & Amsterdam) and Reach partner, Apogee (Hong Kong), created a practice-oriented approach to global UX design that enables design teams and researchers to filter out the most important insights about cultural differences, and apply these in the early stages of their designs. The approach involves a structured way to look at designs through the eyes of people from different cultures, and to make changes based on an understanding of the effect they will have on the user experience. This is not envisaged as an individual design activity, but rather as a structured conversation between UX designers and with other colleagues, such as country managers and localisation teams. Being able to conduct these structured conversations allows UX designers to engage more strategically in design decisions within their company and is therefore sometimes called 'mature UX practice'.

The global design team goals set for the training programme were: to gain an understanding of local perspectives that help to understand similarities and differences that matter for iterative design improvements; to probe conversations in the team about local design nuances and the implications for local design specifics as well as global standards; and to enable a mature global design practice in the organisation, ensuring that the local and global are well represented in an iterative, agile approach to continuous improvement.

To prepare for the training we studied local cultures, current market and design knowledge, and technical user-interface (UI) standards within the organisation. It soon became clear that there was little guidance for interpreting and applying general design examples in local markets. An out-of-the-box global design training was simply not yet available, so this was very much a pioneering effort. We also found that considerable local knowledge was present in pockets around the organisation in presentations and reports, but there was no easy way to extract this local knowledge in a simple way for use in their design practice.

Because of the length and intensity of the training sessions, we devoted special attention to the design of our didactic approach. We sought to avoid excessive cognitive or visual overload, so participants could devote all their energy to the task at hand — practising their conversations on UX design interventions based on meaningful local differences — and not succumb to fatigue as the day progressed.

Guided and structured facilitation by the team from STBY and Apogee helped participants to practice with a range of design examples. Some of these were pre-prepared and others were brought along from projects by participants. The approach was underpinned by a 'global design framework' specially developed for the client organisation in the run-up to the training, in response to the lessons learned from interviewing the design teams.

The instruments developed for the training were a Global Design Playbook that promotes curiosity, interactivity and fun among the design teams, combined with a set of Local Lense Cards. Each of these contains one nugget of local knowledge harvested from existing research into local and global user behaviours. These cards sparked conversations during the training as they were reviewed in relation to the designs by the participants. This approach opened a new perspective for the teams: one where research started to play a different and more strategic role in their global design. Key understandings are now getting a longer life in the organisation, as they are present in day-to-day conversations and decisions in design teams and also between designers and product-owners, marketers, business strategists, and country managers.

Global design should not be seen as a 'trick' that can simply be executed. It requires a mature practice of interpretation, creativity and discussion, based on the acknowledgement that human practice and culture are also always changing, both locally and globally. With the Playbook, the Local Lense Cards and the training programme we have helped the client teams to take an important step towards connecting design and research to form a truly effective global practice. We feel that this new approach could potentially benefit a wider range of organisations that operate on a global scale.

Social innovation programme for international non-governmental organisations

For international non-governmental organisations seeking to proactively manage and drive innovation, the REACH School offers specialised programmes of training and coaching to support ongoing global innovation projects in international non-governmental organisations (INGOs).

An extensive survey among 62 INGOs in 2016 gauged the innovation capacity among them. The findings concluded that the group is in the early stages of their innovation journey and that there is still significant room for consolidation and improvement in how innovation is supported. The research also found that just 14% of survey respondents reported having received formal innovation training, suggesting that INGOs are not proactively seeking to manage and drive innovation[1].

In response to this urgent need, an approach for training and coaching specifically meeting the innovation needs of INGOs was developed by partners from the Reach Network. The programmes take the People-Process-Practice framework as a starting point. As sustainable change requires time and consistent guidance, the programmes deliver a blended learning model that combines thinking and doing in three steps. The first, Launch Pad, introduces participants to basic processes, design tools, methods and templates. Then follows Lift Off, which supplements the basics with direct training from local Reach partners, as well as remote mentorship from global Reach partners (blended learning). Finally, in the Orbit stage at the end of the programme, the knowledge and confidence gained is evaluated and articulated as a practical vision for innovation within the respective organisations.

Learning by doing — social innovation in practice

For some of the major associations of INGOs, STBY has offered practical learning programmes that guide participants through their own social innovation projects in a series of group sessions plus one-to-one coaching. This programme helps innovators in NGOs to take forward their innovation ideas or projects in the organisation. While they progress, they benefit from expert mentoring as well as peer support and challenge. Bespoke guidance and tools are provided to bring about greater impact and more effective initiatives relevant to the issue they are tackling.

The learning programme is specially geared to people who play a key role in helping their organisation to develop new initiatives, design and implement new programmes, or to be more creative, agile and future-fit. As part of their work they are typically involved in initiatives to improve their organisation's programmes, services or processes, and seek to benefit from external inputs. They have already had some experience with the basics of innovation and are eager to take their learning further.

The programme combines a series of half-day group sessions and one-hour individual mentoring sessions over a period of months, to enable the participants to turn their innovation ideas into successful new projects. The group sessions take place at a local venue, while the follow-up coaching uses video conferencing or phonecalls.

The programme makes use of the several bespoke toolkits STBY has developed together with partners in the field. These are used alongside other tools and case studies, to guide participants through a staged process of social innovation, support them to implement the learning back in the workplace, and continue to learn from their experiences as they go through the programme.

The highly experiential programme helps participants to make progress with the specific, real (whether existing or new) projects they have chosen to work on, applying new knowledge and insights to turn their ideas into breakthrough new services and approaches for their organisation. Over the programme they work through the various stages of the innovation process, while receiving custom feedback and suggestions from innovation and service design experts. They also learn from each other by sharing progress in the group sessions, while building a network of peers working on similar challenges. With the aid of the individual mentoring sessions and group sessions, participants work through particular hurdles or issues they are facing.

1   BOND (2016). *The Innovation Audit Big Picture*. Accessed on 3 May from: https://www.bond.org.uk/resources/the-innovation-audit-big-picture-2016

Networked collaborations

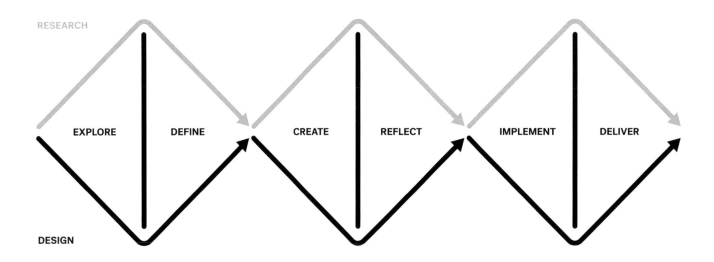

RESEARCH

EXPLORE | DEFINE | CREATE | REFLECT | IMPLEMENT | DELIVER

DESIGN

Supporting global innovation through design research is a very diverse practice, as described and illustrated in this chapter. A large part of the work consists of global design research projects with a clear aim and focus, often done by experienced specialists in collaboration with other stakeholders in global companies and INGOs. A growing part of the work consists of building up global design research capacity across various teams and departments in these organisations, often through a mix of training and coaching on internal projects. This diversity reflects the current state-of-the-art in global design research, which is probably typical for the relatively fledgling state of this field.

The growing need for internal capacity-building points to an increasing interest in strengthening internal expertise in global design research. This is a sign of the growing maturity of the field. We can also see this as a sign that the three networks mentioned at the start of this chapter (networked client organisations, networked agencies, and networked audiences) are becoming increasingly connected. Close collaborations between internal and external design researchers provide strong support for this. We have been pioneering with open and transparent ways of collaborating for many years already,

The underlying framework for the projects and training programmes is based on a 'Triple Diamond' approach. Each stage includes diverging activities, to invite new insights and ideas, as well as converging activities, to ensure a progressive and focused decision making process. In all these stages, research and design are closely intertwined. This approach was informed by the 'Double Diamond' from the UK's Design Council, and extended by STBY to reflect the multi-staged innovation processes we often encounter in industry.

and we have no doubt learned a lot. The next chapter provides examples of this, as it describes a design research practice that has been co-developed while working on a series of international projects with many of our Reach Network partners for one of our large international clients.

PRACTICE

Reflections on disposition and process

THE PRACTICE OF GOOD REASON

Over the course of several years, STBY and the Reach Network collaborated with design researchers Kat Gough and Michael Davis Burchat at one of the largest mobile phone manufacturers in the world, to redevelop its global design research approach. The traditional approach to customer research used within the organisation hitherto had attracted quite some criticism from managers and executives who requested insight about unmet human needs. The complaints were mostly about three generic issues: the lead time required, the complexity of making sense of new information, and the costs of learning about people.

The new design research approach to the requested work touched on a lot of areas, from creating briefs for a series of smaller-scale multi-local design research projects, to the use of its results throughout the organisation — not just in the design organisation, but also in business strategy and marketing. How could we move from a yearly large scale global sweep research that takes the pulse of the planet to a nimbler, more continuous design research effort that would integrate the strategic and creative practices of the organisation? This is the question we were answering, we gradually realised. Nothing less.

We already had found some answers before we realised that this was our question. After all, our approach as pioneers was to learn by doing design research in new ways and reflect on what we achieved and where we had failed, to make sure we progressed our practice over time, bit by bit. More than three years, almost 10 global design research projects and more than 500 short films about people's everyday lives later, we sat down one week in January 2014 in a flat in Beijing to bring our reflections over the years together in what we came to call 'The Practice of Good Reason'.

This Practice relies on collaboration to employ creativity and strategy in balance. Design research sets the groundwork for common conversation, enabling each project to span all disciplines and silos as they step into the unknown. Favouring one silo is not very successful in innovation. As the creator of a design research brief, you may have an overview of where and how your findings may be useful, especially if you work across several parts of a company. You should make use of that higher ground to make the design research more valuable to more people.

Writing up the Practice of Good Reason in a flat in Beijing,
with Michael, Kat Gough, Geke van Dijk (in the foreground)
and Bas Raijmakers (who took this picture).

Any individual commissioning a project is important, but they might not be the only person
working with its findings, or know the most about who else will value the knowledge it produces.
Commissioning a research project around a set of business needs, requests, or departments can suffer
from a range of cognitive biases. When there isn't a clear set of evidence to work from, assumptions
will stand in as a proxy for new knowledge. The Practice of Good Reason creates a preferable body
of evidence to work from, and discards half-truths or workarounds. By extension, the body of evidence
puts us design researchers at the core competence of delivering and learning from that evidence.

The Practice of Good Reason can be summed up in 13 principles that we present here in a linear
order. But this is not a process, nor a manual — these are not 13 steps. As illustrated in four short
essays interspersed between the principles, the 13 principles rather form a scaffold that is systematic
yet flexible. This practice provides enough shared reference points for all participating professionals
to feel confident about their role and the purpose of their contributions, and at the same time
provides space and opportunities for everyone to be inspired and to use their creativity to contribute
to innovative results. These 13 principles express our experience over the years, and the four essays
reflect on some of the underlying themes, such as collaboration and creativity.

Many of these principles are used in every one of our global design research projects with the
Reach Network, such as those described in the case studies in the previous chapter on 'Networks'.
Together, the principles and essays represent our thoughts on how global design research can be done
in a truly human-centred, design-driven and collaborative manner that fits with the networked nature
of today's world. They express the growing maturity of our practice.

13 principles

Define a research topic by identifying a broad area of uncertainty which surrounds the human context

In defining the research topic, you are setting the parameters of a study that will contribute new observations about a particular 'area of uncertainty'. In this stage you are 'problem finding' rather than problem solving. So work towards formulating a single research question that is inquisitive about people and their daily lives. Questions about specific consumer types, technology requirements or business models risk projecting false assumptions into a study. There is no need to rush toward a solution. Design research is interested in investigating research questions from the perspective of anthropology or sociology. A research question that is human-centred will cut across business perspectives, and avoid asking multiple sets of requirement-focused questions taken from across an organisation.

Yet, it should be connected to the organisation by acknowledging a key uncertainty the business has about its strategic intent.

Keep the question open enough to allow for new knowledge to emerge. Additionally, you can define narrower 'lines of enquiry' within the question space, so that the most relevant lines can get studied first. If resources or budget prove to be too limited, some lines of enquiry can be transferred to further rounds of research, findings, and analysis in the future.

For research to contribute effectively to strategic considerations you must provide stakeholders with enough evidence to justify observing, analysing and explaining daily rituals and seemingly mundane activities which surround the usage of a product or

service. In this light, competitive factors and forces of habit must be taken into account. Multiple viewpoints are needed to define a problem before you should rush to solve it. The trick is to do this while avoiding the common pitfalls of assumption, testimony, and business bias in problem solving. 'Business bias' can take many forms, from company structures or segmentation models to media reports or market routes for 'innovative' products.

It is often not possible to discern how new or exciting something is without a benchmark. Keeping this in mind, the research scope doesn't need to exclude common behaviours that people experience, as these may be ultimately relevant to the business and contribute to cutting-edge research in its own right.

Examples of Choosing Methodology

To explore which functionalities of a smart device someone uses most in their everyday lives, we may ask them prior to an interview to sort a stack of cards with discrete functionalities by the level of priority for them, and then ask them to briefly explain their top five cards. This will give an indication of which functionalities to further explore in-depth during the interview, and what situations to capture on 'film'.

To support the richness and precision of people's accounts of their practices and motivations around their smart devices, we ask them to 're-enact' an everyday routine using a particular functionality on their device. This physical re-enactment of a daily routine, and the reflective account about it as a 'show & tell' often triggers accounts of details that may appear trivial but turn out to be key during analysis, when we compare routines across research participants.

Propose and structure your research by considering different ways to investigate people's behaviour

An important objective is to match the defined research topic to research methods that are most suited to investigating and capturing the behaviours and motivations of interest, within the scope of the uncertainty. Additionally, you should seek ways to control against the risk of believing what you wanted to hear. This is also the time to determine how many people to invite as research participants and to define the range of human experiences they can represent. Define criteria for recruitment and selection, as well as how often to meet with the participants and in what context to do so. Several 'lines of inquiry' can be arrayed to decide how and when to engage with participants.

Not all stakeholders will understand or be aware of human-centred methods for inquiry, which can mean they are left confused, intimidated or easily overwhelmed by the expert knowledge

needed. The model of Citizen Science presents a useful way to separate the work of experts from the work of everybody. Design researchers working in a core team perform the work they are familiar with, such as designing a question, writing a protocol, shadowing a participant or stimulating a conversation. Stakeholders will be called upon later, once these data are ready to examined and analyzed.

It is important to form a core team that is able to collaborate closely during the work. This can be a core group of design researchers, but it can also include those from other disciplines with the proviso that they participate fully in all aspects of the process. The core team can be as small as one or two, but don't find team members to participate part-time, or increase the team size unnecessarily. Collaborate to jointly anticipate what kind of situations you are aiming to investigate and

capture — this will help to anticipate everyone's roles in fieldwork and identify your research methodology.

Creativity plays an important role at this stage, as it informs the choice of your bespoke methodology, impacting the project's process and outcomes. These creative and strategic decisions revolve around maintaining a balance between rigour (required steps and activities) and customisation (what really works best in this context, with these participants, for this topic, and for an audience from the wider organisation?). A creative approach to defining the project methodology sits in stark contrast to simply following an existing research procedure, and recreating a method that has been used before. If you want to delve deeper and find new insights from a different angle, you'll need to do more than just replicating an old trick in the book.

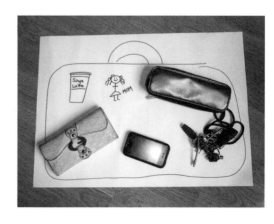

PRINCIPLE #3

Observe situations and events by capturing on film how people think about and act upon the topic

Prepare for fieldwork by selecting participants, writing an interview guide, and having discussions within the core team and the wider organisation. These preparations are collaborative, helping to further describe and understand the research space, lines of inquiry, or behaviours of interest.

Preparations for fieldwork, in particular interviews, need to translate the language of the organisation into words that fit with the world of the participants. It takes creative collaboration between the design researcher and the client to formulate how to connect social science with engineering or implementation. This process continues in the fieldwork, which makes it beneficial to have the same design researchers from both the agency and client present at each visit to continue the conversation.

Once in the field during visits with participants, the aim is to collect 'stories' about their activities and then effectively communicate them in the best possible way to meet the needs of your audience within the team or organisation. Film is an ideal medium for this, allowing this audience to later step into the shoes of the participants, looking at their world from their perspective.

After getting an overview of what stories could be told by a participant, you can then select two to three stories to explore further. Choose these stories based on the research scope, remaining sensitive to 'unknown unknowns'. Filming these stories is a collaboration between the participant and design researchers. The participants contribute to how the story is told and filmed through observation, interviews, and re-enactment.

The design researchers film the story with a rough editing scheme that emerges during the visit, allowing for an initial analysis during fieldwork. Ideally, two design researchers film these stories together, as they can discuss during the visit and bring different perspectives to the story. One design researcher should focus on interacting directly with the participant and leading the conversation. The other design researcher can take more of an observer's role, shooting additional material, and asking extra questions at the end.

This fieldwork results in film material of two to three stories related to the overall research question and lines of inquiry, as well as written descriptive notes and photographs that allow for a rich profile of the participant, showing their activities, motivations and context as well as themselves, through highly visual material.

Opening
up
silos

Silo walls in large organisations are often erected as a way to amplify the creativity of each particular division in isolation. As such, they have the unfortunate effect of producing different accounts about the outside world. Such differences in belief will not always reassemble when coherence is needed to manage the whole of the business.

It took a small core team of research experts to design ways to remove the burden of working with design research methods — and evidence. That burden weighed particularly on stakeholders who were new to human-centred methods. Once the burden could actually be lifted, design documentaries offered a neutral platform for the world to come together with. And for the making of shared discoveries with. Discoveries that could be owned by the company. Not the silo. After which, collaboration became more inviting than argumentative.

Successful collaborations produced new reasons to trust. And in turn, new bonds of trust produced the urge for either deeper or broader acts of collaboration. Stakeholders learned to intuit what parts of the outside world they were not deeply aware of. They also learned to ask for fresh evidence to work with, to be delivered in harmony with their deadlines and planning timeframes. As managers and executives made gentle discoveries about the outside world, they felt encouraged to propose new lines of inquiry that fell within the broader 'area of (corporate) uncertainty'.

Another side effect of silos acting upon a single model of the world was agility. Sense-making conversations learned to evolve rapidly. Replacing prior ideas about project lead times that had become such an issue. Once narrower lines of inquiry were framed in consistency with previous ones, new knowledge built upon a common

Silos provide large organisations with ways to make decisions, and to assign who gets the last word on any decision made. Still, even the most decisive organisation will struggle to attain creativity in the long term. How might advances in collaboration amplify the production of creativity?

platform for Good Reason. The costs of research shrank. And fresh evidence was made available after two-week sprints, rather than the eight-month expeditions that stakeholders were accustomed to.

Removing the burden of participating in a design-research analysis workshop had the effect of moving the collaborative work to the front end work of problem finding.

The core team flexed and evolved throughout each stage of the global design research.
In defining the research brief, the collaborative multi-disciplinary team also asked, "How can we design a brief that takes into account how and where the findings may be useful to others across several parts of an organisation?"

In this way, the collaborative team engaged wider disciplines in design, product management, executive leadership, marketing or engineering as a route to setting lines of inquiry and conducting research. Furthermore, they engaged wider disciplines over time, not only to understand how/when/why they needed to incorporate research into design decisions, but also to collaborate on research documentation that is inclusive of their practice and role in creative design decisions.

After all, design research wasn't just about answering to the individual commissioning the project, but to all of those who may work with the findings in the future, in various ways, in response to various design and development briefs.

PRINCIPLE #4

Select and exclude evidence by jointly reviewing your film material

Some parts of the archive of edited films will produce more knowledge than other parts do. Make notes about what can be learned (by the company) about each research participant's experience as you re-watch the film material that was gathered during fieldwork. Apply a label for the selected fragments. This inventory of labeled fragments provides a way for managing current and future projects.

Significant observations will be depicted in each selected fragment, but extra contextual details and interpretation can be valuable. Sort the film material into 'fragments' that roughly match your 'lines of inquiry'. These 'fragments' are short clips that form the basis for your films that will be edited later. Often there are many 'fragments' that can be edited into films, so they need to be reviewed and the

most relevant and interesting selected. Using a 'matrix' overview that lists 'fragments' per participant and matches them against the 'lines of enquiry' can help to make this selection.

Hold joint conversations within the core team about the contents and meaning of each fragment. At this point, interesting insights in relation to your lines of inquiry become apparent, and you can see which data in your material is memorable, surprising, or already well known. Ask each other: "Is there something there?"

Look for the 'real and relevant' in your insights. Ask yourself, "Is this really part of daily life?" Niche and fringe are interesting, but you are looking for the routine and commonplace in practices and behaviour. Stay collaborative and consistent, by sharing the materials and questioning emerging insights

among the research team, opening up discussion and debate. It helps to work with the same team of design researchers throughout this process, starting at the beginning with fieldwork preparations.

A large part of this process is interpretive, yet ethical. Be honest and respectful to the participants' stories and how they share them with you. Learn to interpret only what can be observed. You should at all times feel comfortable to present the stories you create to the research participants, even though you might never do so.

Should a fragment seem missing, consider why you are not seeing a certain lens on the experience. Such questions will take you back to the field in search of new situations to record.

	At Home	At Work	In Transit	At One	At Large
Mobile Computing					
Connected Life					
Connected Entertainment					
Work-in-Life					

PRINCIPLE #5

Maintain different perspectives on your films by summarising film fragments together

'AEIOU'[1] is an example of a helpful way of categorising that invites you to see film fragments through five different lenses: the 'Activity' of an individual, the 'Environment' of use (how place influences the situation or experience), the nature of 'Interaction' among people, the 'Object' used in the situation, and how the 'Users' observed themselves, their motives, attitudes or responsibilities.

It helps to work in a small group and use tools like 'AEIOU' to review these film fragments together and explain them to each other, one fragment at a time. The work of analysing video fragments collectively as a group produces the effect of a deeper awakening about how people experience situations. At the same time this part of the Practice represents the interchange of interpretation and questioning between the core team and the larger body of stakeholders.

It is also helpful to summarise what takes place in each fragment — if possible, by using only a single sentence. When people within an organisation who have different backgrounds observe the same situations, they will see each one differently, and these differences in perspective are helpful, contributing to a 'thick description'[2] of human context. This description takes an expansive, elaborated view of a particular film fragment, recording new knowledge on these observations in a structured manner that enables easy use and re-use.

1 Robinson, R., Prokopoff, I., Cain, J., Pokorny, J. (1991) *AEIOU*. Doblin group, Chicago. See http://help.ethnohub.com/guide/aeiou-framework
2 Geertz, C. (1973) *The Interpretation of Cultures*. New York, Basic Books.

Collaborative discovery

Close collaboration was crucial to the success of global design research that operated across client and agency networks, often around the world. Once a project was commissioned, collaboration was not just among team members of the organisation, but also between the organisation and the agency to work together in the design, formulation, and development of the brief. Often, agencies are employed as short-term extra labour for a fixed-term, fixed-fee contract, in order to deliver specific answers to a business problem. Through the creation of a core collaborative team, with daily/weekly meetups, decision making and sharing sessions, we avoided an 'over the fence' approach of research questions and answers. In fact, the collaborative team also avoided the idea of 'research answers' altogether by having shared goals in problem finding, analysing behaviours in context and communicating knowledge.

When research is classified as a part of product and service development, its timescale and processes tend to be set in stone, with planned iterations and gates; there is an assumption about the depth of the business question(s) that are feasible to ask within set 'milestones'. Collaborative teamwork opened up space for negotiating from more rigid timeframes led to a process that allowed more flexibility and iterative analysis within a changing design or business context — one that better suited ongoing research in support of product, service or portfolio development. In this way the Design Researcher role also became one of Curator, for not only the questions, topics or regions to be observed, but also for the evidence gathered, collated and analysed (see Inclusive Documentation below).

In collaboration with the agency, it was key that at least one person from the client organisation was deeply involved in the overall design research process, taking part in all the

On teaming with a wide range
of multidisciplinary people
from the client organisation
and the agency, who can meet
and work together regularly to
build a shared understanding
and approach to the work

stages and helping to make considered decisions. This person had ownership and decision-making power over the project. Not only because this strongly informed strategic choices being made throughout the design research project (e.g. what to further explore, emphasise, leave out), but also because it was crucial for the use and acceptance of the research outcomes in the organisation. This client involvement was different from the more traditional way of inviting people from the wider client team to visit parts of the fieldwork just to get a flavour of it, as they are then merely 'design research tourists' rather than key members of the design research team.

The client leads seeking agency collaboration looked for a partner that demonstrated the importance of collecting neutral evidence to a company's business interests, staying true to a person's life and culture. The agency communicated their findings without a projection of who people are or what they want, and were able to facilitate multiple parties with differing business practices and objectives. Lastly, they were able to ask questions to understand where company rhetoric or assumptions may have crept in along the way. These needs represented a type of collaboration that was based on trust and respect for each other's professionalism, rather than the typical power relations between client organisation and agency, and between silos in an organisation. If this respect and trust is achieved, and grows over time, the quality and impact of the global design research will grow too.

Participants & Films CHINA	THE FIVE LINES OF INQUIRY					purchase considerations	ecosystem of devices	social environment	phone as a material object
	Camera Use	Sensing the environment	Micro Tasks	Handling Content	Effect of environment				
Participant 1									
1. Capturing a photo of my dog to share this moment with my husband	X		X	X					
2. Switching between Dictionary and messaging to communicate			X	X				X	
3. Not able to listen to my podcasts on my phone			X	X			X		
Participant 2									
1. Cleaning my phone and give it another life					X		X		X
2. Checking if Bear is coming home for dinner		X	X					X	
3. Why Bear chose her Dad's phone for and teaching him to use the phone						X			X
Participant 3									
1. I can't use my phone for work other than calls and SMSing			X	X		X	X		
2. Issues & frustrations with my phone		X	X		X				X
Participant 4									
1. Morning Routines			X				X		
2. Setting up Stock Application on phone			X	X		X			
Participant 5									
1. Prefer a writing pad on my phone		X	X			X		X	
2. Don't know how to send a phone number from my phone's address book			X	X					
Participant 6									
1. Saturday morning breakfast rituals at McDonalds before meeting friends			X	X	X		X	X	
2. Learning English using the dictionary on my phone			X	X	X				
3. Taking a photo, giving it a personal touch and sharing with my friends	X			X				X	
4. Comparing my two phones						X		X	X
Participant 7									
1. Getting work instructions from my boss			X	X	X				
2. Comparing my current and previous phones						X			X
Participant 8									
1. Having trouble entering text on my phone		X							X
2. My old mobile phones and why I'm keeping them						X	X		X

PRINCIPLE #6

Prepare evidence for use and re-use by editing and organising films into a catalogue and library

The process of film editing resembles the process of qualitative data analysis; it is collaborative, iterative, and requires both time and patience. The large repository of roughly-sorted data (interview fragments, observed context, re-enacted practices) needs to be slowly processed into coherent, meaningful stories. During fieldwork and the first stage of analysis, the understanding of these practices and behaviours of interest grow, and the stories you can tell around them become clearer. This process benefits from collaboration; by showing the work and reflecting on it together, you can strengthen how you tell these stories to others.

Critically watching and re-watching the films helps you get closer to the participant's stories, their practice(s), and the motivations they share behind it, which all guide the film editing. This process is not just about creating an engaging story; it is guided by how to best express the experiences and point of view of the participant, rather than that of the editor. It helps to compare behaviours and motivations across research participants by working on a series of films at the same time, enabling you to refine the individual story in each film.

A written-up documentation of findings, such as participant profiles, is a crucial outcome of the editing process in addition to these films. Documentation provides context to the films and a foundation to the 'trail of evidence' that grounds your insights. This grounding is essential, allowing you to go between observations on individual behaviour and synthesised insights on behavioural patterns across the sample. The material generated during this analysis needs to provide for this trail of evidence, as it is used as input for future workshops; it needs to allow for people who have not been involved in the fieldwork to join in this process of analysis, collaboration, and documentation.

PRINCIPLE #7

Analyse your evidence from multiple perspectives by holding a collaborative workshop

The first workshop after fieldwork is a chance to begin to analyse the evidence, and is the first of many iterations. The outcome of this first workshop isn't to produce a set of insightful 'answers' to the questions that client stakeholders and agency design researchers have asked before and during the fieldwork, but to use the evidence provided in films to define a common ground among different disciplines and departments. Bringing in wider team members from different disciplines into this workshop is very useful, aligning multiple perspectives and preventing the restriction of a team's interest. By sharing the practice of observing and discussing the data, more of the company can be brought together in empathy for the experiences of their consumers. During the workshop, a shared lexicon evolves to express people's activities, needs and motivations in the world, without relying on pre-existing company assumptions or conforming to pre-existing business 'knowns'. This is documented in an accessible, inclusive way to extend the value of this lexicon beyond the workshop itself (see Inclusive Documentation below).

During the workshop, it is best if people can set aside their particular department's deliverables, and refrain from contributing personal anecdotes. Throughout the process of looking at the data and drawing insights, the trick is to avoid the inclusion of assumptions and myths from around the company. During discussion of the film material, participants may bring to the table specific knowledge of company constraints which can help to form and deepen evidence and identify topics and problem areas to explore further.

The discussion should be based on a clear 'trail of evidence,' ensuring that insights and topics of discussion are founded in and justified by the data, as opposed to being from personal interest. Workshop materials should also include sufficient documentation to understand and work with this 'trail of evidence,' so that people can trace observations and insights back to individual participants, and use it to substantiate their own ideas and insights.

Documentation of the workshop results should also provide a 'trail of evidence,' allowing others not present to trace back ideas and insights, and understand what observed behaviour and expressed motivations the insights are based on. Outcomes from this first workshop can already be useful for those across the company to take more evidence from real lives into the decision-making process, whether they are a planner, engineer, designer, marketer, or developer.

Iterative Delivery

A paradox at the root of this project began naively enough, with the posing of a question. Might a company be able to learn more, by working with less? Rather than deliberate further, the core team were in the field within four business days to gather fresh evidence. Radical, when compared with a 19-week lead time we needed to replace. To seasoned researchers it was not surprising that we were finding a bounty of new knowledge from these first re-enactments. What was going unnoticed, however, was the tacit ease with which we chose to move forward and chose to backup, in the processes of our work. How might an outsider to the process learn the dance steps we were now taking for granted? At first this felt difficult to prepare an amateur for.

There were, for instance, reasons to dive back into evidence, or even revisit a participant, if we discovered that an area of uncertainty needed further explanation, or a theme emerged that shed new light on an earlier observation. This was true for the core research team,

but also for other people from the wider organisation who could step in at any stage and bring wider interpretations with them.

This iterative notion about delivery shaped the ways we built up research knowledge incrementally and affordably across locations and regions, as prompted by the emerging demands of every new stakeholder. In a prior era of research, securing approval for one massive multi-continent research was presenting risks of cost, complexity and lethargy. The problems of speed and scale now appeared fixable. But how might we mitigate organisational complexity? We would resolve to decouple intake of new evidence from the output of new findings. Enabling new clients to request fresh evidence, or to extract knowledge as independent acts.

Examining human experiences in depth, region by region, meant that hypotheses were built over time. No less valid or rigorous, since they were more closely

On being always open to look forward and backward across the stages of research to review and explore any stage of the process again with fresh eyes.

associated with the organisation's design intentions. Earlier analysis could simply acknowledge more uncertainties or assumptions, and frame any problem space with greater clarity and focus over time. Research and analysis no longer needed to happen at the start of a design, development, or product management process. Rarely was there a clean slate to work from to begin with. The Practice of Good Reason, with time, would learn to focus on consequent entry and exit to the work of each stakeholder *who engaged us*.

Producing *communicable observations* continually throughout the work was elementary to a research practice that fostered iteration rather intuitively. Because film fragments contained modules of knowledge. And modules of knowledge were ready-made for assembly, and re-iteration. Capturing evidence on film or as descriptions created material that had longevity during the research and beyond. Behaviours captured on film were framed to be interpreted in the moment, and also re-analysed over subsequent years. Providing a faster, cheaper, deeper method of design research for producing knowledge with. Knowledge that was often stable for a seven to ten year horizon.

Iterative models of delivery assured deeper discoveries within rapid response times. Social complexity was no longer feared by design research. Stakeholders were socially free to interact whenever a key uncertainty about customers emerged to them. Or when organisational changes ushered in changes to a design agenda, a product roadmap, a communications plan or a worthy problem.

PRINCIPLE #8

Make outcomes rich and grounded by referencing particular evidence

Workshop documentation should highlight the collaborative analysis of observational evidence, linking particular well-referenced evidence to clusters of observation. This documentation provides a way of summarising evidence in order to create a shared understanding across teams and departments. By presenting the shared analysis and lexicon that describes activities and needs, it provides a tangible reminder of the original evidence, of shared observations, and of the relevance it has for their organisation, while avoiding the tethering of one observation to only one business need.

Documentation should avoid providing a 'chocolate box' of sensational, tasty 'insight treats' which can become distorted as they travel around a business, losing their connection to the original evidence. Where documentation can go astray is when it is considered as an end in itself, a report to justify time, money, and resources spent in fieldwork. A set of insights from fieldwork is then forced to stand alone, before they are incorporated into other analytical processes or used with other data.

Research departments and agencies can sometimes be encouraged at this stage to increase the impact of 'insightful' reports that have a 'ta-dah' delivery. Insights may then be expressed as concrete conclusions, rather than as purely observational research, which can estrange the evidence from its conclusions and let prior business assumptions to linger and remain uncorrected. The significance of well crafted and evidenced conclusions is to spur clients to reframe a biased view point.

Capture, Review & Share
Insights & Opportunities

...STBY...

PRINCIPLE #9

Distinguish moments of human need by interpreting the difficulty and uncertainty of an activity

The main question to ask here is: what uncertainties and difficulties do participants in the research have? Uncertainties are important because they may cause people to not even try to accomplish or operate something, while difficulties are important because they may cause people to fail in what they try to accomplish or operate.

With recurring and relevant activities and tasks, there are generally five dimensions to the interpretation of uncertainties and difficulties:

Physical Can the person physically operate the feature, device or do the task, not only in the lab but also in his/her situation?

Cognitive How does the person understand the feature, device or the task, what knowledge does s/he use?

Emotional How does the person feel about using the feature, device or doing the task?

Social How does the activity fit in the person's social fabric?

Cultural How does the activity fit in the person's culture?

It's also important that to establish the activities and operations observed are relevant and recurring in people's lives. To analyse what makes the user uncertain and activities they find difficult to perform is to identify user needs which have significant impact in their lives.

Allow for transparency in the claims you make as a result of your interpretation and analysis, grounding your concepts in observed and analysed

practices; this creates a strong evidence base. Design teams can sometimes 'dip into' analysed evidence randomly, picking an insight to support a prior held hypothesis, but this clouds the ability to benchmark and compare concepts developed through the research.

Systematic, structured and grounded analysis offers relevant examples and context to inform and inspire business, design and marketing. The creativity needed in each of these disciplines can be made 'apparent' through the varied interpretations that their practitioners have (see Apparent Creativity below). All sources and associations of their creativity should be made 'apparent' for collaborators to learn from or scrutinize.

Documenting for Inclusion

The social life of information can be secretive, repetitive, and evolutionary. These are the starting criteria that stakeholders began with. Document formats change as often as their content does. If design research was going to capture, explain, and facilitate interpretations, how were we to balance our need for discipline with their demand for customization? Our role would be to produce ingredients of the best quality, but never to act as the cook in the kitchen. This social boundary helped us to work inclusively while respecting a stakeholders' autonomy about how to document their own deliverables.

On other occasions we compared our work of selecting, and organizing research or analysis to that of curating a library. A library that was expanding with new topics, about people from ever wider regions and with knowledge that was increasing in depth. At issue was a search for a common unit of evidence/film to curate: How might we select a relatively consistent amount of information to be analysed? And how would that choice feel intuitive to work with?

We knew that we needed to have systematic consistency to make the library, which consisted of data gathered during different research phases, in different regions by different teams, consistent over time. Global design research needs a consistent frame-work for documenting evidence as the research expands in volume, to create comparability across observations.

The optimal span of attention during the workshops also determined the common unit of evidence/film. Our stakeholders were all competent with the quantitative reasoning that relies on formulae from algebra or calculus. Workshops, unlike meetings, facilitate ways of analysing qualitative evidence. Would this help them adapt to the qualitative practices that rely on frameworks from anthropology or sociology? Eventually we limited each unit of film to three minutes or less.

Within a Design Documentary[1], a person from the outside world speaks to the camera and thinks aloud while re-enacting a recent experience. This form of documentation produced a visceral effect in the viewer, triggering deeper associations about the purpose of a technology. Comparative representations of the same information (verbatim text, personae, or information diagrams), by contrast, required more work on the part of a stakeholder.

Workshops enabled a wider audience to observe the user's experience first hand through short films, and demonstrated how the environment, context of use, or interface could disable an activity. An audience from business or design were able to identify strongly with a problem. Situating the benefits and frustrations for people during their activities contributed to a discussion within teams that revolved around benefits, rather than features.

Frameworks such as AEIOU[2] enabled stakeholders to devote deeper attention to actions, behaviours or tasks, together with the environments, interactions and tools that surround an experience. It also allowed the audience to make comparisons outside prior held assumptions,

On gathering and presenting evidence
continually using an accessible
manner, such that others not directly
involved with the project can
understand materials and engage
with evidence at any point.

providing insight across age, ability or segmentation categories. It emphasised technology as a means to an end, rather a fleeting declaration of attitude, which would have been less informative to a product manager, designer or developer.

Without needing to understand how an observation and rich evidence was captured, an audience could watch and get engaged with user behaviour, recognising issues with activities that they themselves or other users do. As a result, they started championing the user experience in decision-making.

We used 'thick description'[3] to describe activities and behaviours, in order to deepen our study. As different areas of the problem space were researched, the compatibility of observations helped to provide robustness, flexibility and interesting viewing in the analysis, to the point that some new questions from the design team would not require fresh primary research.

The development of a shared language around a project also helps those taking part to play strong roles as 'apparent creatives' (see essay below) in the design and development process. Throughout the project a team creates a shared lexicon to discuss the problem space, observations, evidence and ideas. They build this together on an ongoing basis, with reference to original evidence from the research to avoid implicit assumptions.

The business of curating which units/modules to analyse fell to the core team. The business of observing, explaining and decoding human behaviors, phenomena,

and motives, meanwhile, were drawn out of members of the extended team. Each member brought a differing logic and disposition to bear on a collective 'thick description' of the outside world.

Additionally, insights were summarised into longer 'compilation films' demonstrating which human needs or uncertainties would make analysis quickly accessible and apparent across the organisation.

One positive side effect of building a library of evidence was that we could rapidly host an evidence workshop with little overhead or lead time. Reaching this level of maturity naturally increased the rate at which designs, strategies, and even acquisitions were based on this Practice of Good Reason.

An inclusive approach to documentation never sought to complicate research methods or mystify everyday life. We avoided opaque practices which might sensationalise or give disproportionate weight to an opportunity.

1   Raijmakers, B. (2007). *Design Documentaries*. PhD thesis Royal College of Art, London. See designdocumentaries.com
2   Robinson, R., Prokopoff, I., Cain, J., Pokorny, J. (1991) *AEIOU*. Doblin group, Chicago. See http://help.ethnohub.com/guide/aeiou-framework
3   Geertz, C. (1973) *The Interpretation of Cultures*. New York, Basic Books.

PRINCIPLE #10

Decode the state of the art for gaps by comparing and contrasting human needs with industry norms

All industries can get swept up in a biased view of the world, informed by trends and reports of technological process in a particular industry. Researchers should look at the state of the art for ways that technology disagrees or misaligns with the daily lives of their research participants; this will enable a company or organisation to assess the relevance of its products and services to potential or expected users.

As the research helps the question "What makes activities difficult for people to perform?", certain human factors are identified. These inform

the analysis of 'competitive forces' — which are alternative available features, services or accessories that the user might seek out instead. In shared design discussions, competitive forces that may be difficult to trump in terms of technology can be easier to compete with in terms of a product or service's usefulness, convenience, usability, reliability, or meaning to people.

By searching for existing technologies intended to service particular activities or needs, as end users might themselves, it is possible to analyse a technological concept for its

technical properties and functionality. Explain each technology with a two-part description that answers the questions: what component(s) is the technology made of? What does it do for people?

This analysis will help to identify gaps between human uncertainty and difficulty, and the functional properties of current or new technologies. You should suspend judgment of a concept prior to analysing and explaining the meaningful matches and mismatches between a particular technology, its intended functionality, and its observed usage.

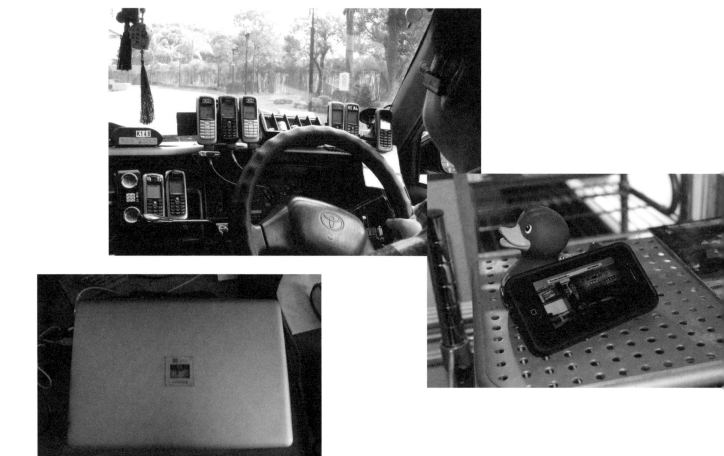

PRINCIPLE #11

Close the gap between inventions and innovations by devising ways to service unmet needs

Problem finding is a critical step in solving 'worthy problems' —those that are actually experienced in the life of a user or consumer. In order to generate a list of 'worthy problems', we must compare what a technology promises to do, its competitive force, with what consumers appear to struggle with, the human factor.

When explaining technologies as tools that facilitate better features, services or products, it helps to source or develop technology that will serve as a means to an end. Or as a means to achieving a (human) purpose.

In order to create factors that lead to differentiation in the marketplace, and ideas that differ from the industry norm, we must generate requirements which are grounded in a knowledge gap. This knowledge gap is informed by the design research, 'design factors' and 'competitive forces' identified and refined during workshops. As design and development teams work generatively to create concepts, these concepts can be tested through a 'means test' which can also be described as 'the job to be done'[1] — that represents how well the job gets done from one technology concept choice as opposed to another.

Teams across companies, whether executive, strategy, product, or implementation planning, often proceed towards 'competitiveness', assuming the continual demand for 'today's state of the art, tomorrow'. This approach can fail people in a range of significant ways. Value can instead be generated with creativity in problem finding, throughout the various teams in an organisation.

1   Christensen, C., Dillon, K., Hall, T., Duncan, D. (2016). Know Your Customers' "Jobs to Be Done". In: Harvard Business Review, September 2016. See also https://hbr.org/2016/09/know-your-customers-jobs-to-be-done

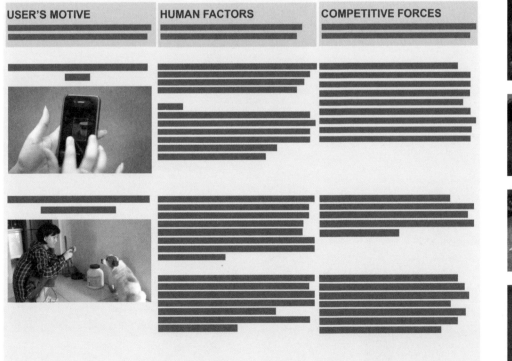

USER'S MOTIVE   HUMAN FACTORS   COMPETITIVE FORCES

PRINCIPLE #12

Generate elements of a preferable system by translating unmet needs into functionalities

Once the 'problem-to-solve' has been summarised as a 'job-to-be-done', this can be re-written as a call to action: "How might we enable people to perform" the <job-to-be-done> <under the conditions of uncertainty and difficulty>?
Project team members from all disciplines can brainstorm and generate lists of possible ways to fulfil the call to action. If 100 to 150 possibilities are generated, this is enough to both achieve competitiveness and to create value with.

The ideas can then be arranged into clusters, with each cluster being summarised and worked with as a plausible concept or means to fulfil the user's purpose. Each summary can be expanded with just enough detail: what is the minimal set of system elements required to fulfil the user's purpose? What does each element of the system do for the benefit of the user?
Ideas can be both wild and predictable, mixing written explanations with visual depictions. Working generatively benefits from a mixture

of laughter and joking, and a ban on the censorship of a proposed idea — motivating everyone in the production of ideas.
Good Reason Practice remains relevant to teams through concept development by promoting topics grounded in human needs with a framework that can provide scaffolding throughout the design and development process. The human factors and success measures support features, products and services that can remain relevant to human needs for longer.

PRINCIPLE #13

Show the benefit to a consumer by highlighting how an offering connects to their needs and values

Bringing a new device, feature, app, or service to market can and should remain connected to the behaviour and motivations observed during fieldwork. The deep understanding of the consumer generated through the Good Reason Practice reveals what it is about this new offering that will resonate with the user or consumer. Chosen features and functionalities are a direct response or solution to the difficulties and uncertainties observed.

A difficulty at this stage is that advertising is focused on target markets and consumer segments, even though this may not be the best way to describe consumers. Audiences are now fragmented beyond a segmentation that is purely sociodemographic, and

people combine different behaviours that do not fit within one particular segment. For example, an Indian retiree, an American mother, and a Chinese teenage may all have the same need in a particular aspect of their lives. It may be possible to advertise value that they feel attracted to because of their needs and motivations in one fell swoop, as opposed to through three different avenues.

Products or services that result from this process connect directly to observed difficulties or behaviours, understood and analysed, and become criteria that can be used to measure the success of certain offerings on the market. They should be advertised as addressing these difficulties or

uncertainties people have, as opposed to targeting specific customer segments. Visual advertising can build on the fieldwork documentation, expressing the value and meaning of a new offering, and its connection to observed daily life, needs, values, and motivations.

By using fewer aspirational and lifestyle cues to attract a target set of consumers we hope to connect with, it is possible to demonstrate benefits of the experience, product or service developed, so that people to make accurate deductions, rather than hoping that a brand reputation will deliver. Good reasoning provides clear evidence and analysis of what people value and how new or different it will be to them.

Apparent Creativity

We never set about to define modes of creativity. Our mission was to supply new knowledge *to* creativity as if it were a single mode of thought. Still, the generally accepted idea of creativity often conflates your identity with your competence. We realised that design research creates a heightened awareness about *how* you create and what *ought* to be created, resulting in two practical definitions of creativity. The first is commonly accepted. The latter represents an important discovery for organisations in search of change.

In a cognitive sense, the experience of creativity feels the same to the scientist, the designer, and the engineer. Creativity is not what we ask others to do for us. Creativity represents how our minds change as we grow — making it hard to defend the argument that some disciplines are creative, while others are not. We report that discoveries made during this effort were 'authored by groups' of people rather than individuals. Groups composed of executives, leaders, managers, and specialists. Individuals who do not normally *identify* as 'the creative type'.

The original symptoms of lethargy, soaring costs, and sclerotic decision making, were traced back to a feint in direction, when one silo acted without creative access to another for an extended period of time. Ideas generated in isolation only took longer for all silos to ratify.

We point out that these two modes of practice can overlap amicably. Recall that a core team of design researchers relieved an extended team of the creative burden of gathering field research. Inversely, the extended team was able to request further lines of inquiry, relieving the core team of the creative burden of imagining all that needed to be discovered in an extensive study. In this example, members of each team operated in both modes.

Creativity is needed throughout the data collection, to share initial hypothesis and thoughts and bring these elements to the forefront in stories from participants. Creativity is then needed to craft these real stories together with the participants, which has relies on individual and collaborative modes. Each individual has their own creative contribution to the process — whether it's operating the video camera, speaking about their experiences, or taking contextual photographs. Once it is not only the people commonly perceived as 'creatives' who do this work, and your team is rich in multiple logics, then the urges

An exclusive and enclosed approach
to a creative process which obscures
the generative sources and associations
used to produce a new idea, as if
to appear from a black box or resemble
magic. — Opaque creativity

An inclusive and open approach to
a creative process which explains or
clarifies the generative sources and
associations used to produce a new idea,
as if to invite the critical thinking
of many authors. — Apparent creativity

to stereotype and fictionalise the life of a customer disappear quite naturally.

The Practice model we share here worked in a variety of ways to sidestep tired cliches about lone-inventors: the light-bulbs that appear to them, the viral sensation their hit product created, the influence that hipsters had on the rest of the world in producing that sensational effect. Every depiction of creativity in popular culture is fraught with cliches about an epiphany. Apparent creativity provides you with a preferable alternative. Perceived losses in autonomy are quickly compensated with a richer and clearer model of the world. Plain language turned out to be the active ingredient in the Practice of Good Reason. By reducing the use of hyperbole and sensationalism, the Practice was easy, even for skeptics, to adopt.

The organisation that *hired us* needed external assurance about how to make deep changes which would stand the test of time. Looking back on this objective, it was achieved in two parts. A usable body of qualitative knowledge, and an open and inclusive way of converting that knowledge into new ideas/designs. In other words, the knowledge and practice for stimulating collective creativity.

Once this way of working stabilised, questions emerged about how rapidly its validity might perish. Is there an expiry date on empathy?

We learned that behaviours in one part of the world were enriched by observations from very different cultures. We also learned to re-visit participants to see how their behaviours were evolving. By grounding the problems in human behaviour, members of the extended team could focus on enduring issues and the functional purpose of a product — not the unsubstantiated technology predictions of a pundit, for whom the pace of change appears to be short and accelerating.

Given enough time, the evidence we gathered using longitudinal rigour, indicated that behavioural models retain anthropological relevance in a corporate setting for periods of seven to ten years.

Not all organisations seek change. For some organisations, the status quo provides growth and stability in equilibrium. This practice model is suited to the businesses, and the external agencies who service them, that need to make significant step into the unknown.

The authors on the Great Wall.

A mature practice

The Practice of Good Reason, which we have gradually developed over the last six years, has proven to be a way of working that ensures inclusion and shared experience between both design and research teams, as well as together with more technical, business or marketing-oriented teams. We have used this practice in both the private and public sectors, as well as in academia.

One thing that has consistently occurred within those shared experiences is the teams gaining much confidence and experience of analysing, co-designing and presenting ideas at the close of the engagement.

In part, we believe this relates to increased collaborative work with participants, and time spent observing and empathising with their needs. This offers teams the opportunity to brush up on or learn new techniques in design research during the project. The practice of Good Reason supports a co-design process for which prior design training is not necessarily required.

We've seen ideas form collaboratively and confidently with shared reference to evidence, or build over time with shared knowledge about their origin. Shared language has helped teams discuss ideas and take quick decisions together, or to build new thoughts onto existing evidence whilst retaining a connection with the original idea.

LANDSCAPES

Design and innovation in a networked world

DESIGNING FOR MEANING

Most products and services are born to satisfy some sort of human need, though many of these were not created by people with the job title of 'designer' or 'inventor'. Instead, they were locally developed to fulfil the everyday needs of all kinds of different people. Fast forward to the modern day, and things are not quite the same. Strategy, design and development have become more concentrated into the hands of the few, creating for the very many. When those designers and strategists are not close to the people who they are creating for, they are less empathetic to the contexts in which the products will be used, simply because they are less familiar with how people give meanings to things in the communities in which they live.

The forces of globalisation are also shaking all of this up[1]. Firstly, in many parts of the world, local communities have become a lot more diverse. Metropolitan neighbourhoods are no longer homogenous clusters of like-minded and alike-looking people. Italian-British households sit alongside Korean-French ones, eating Greek food and driving Japanese cars. What would before have been referred to as a local community is now, in fact, a microcosm of the world. In line with Said and Anderson, communities and geographies, both local and global, are being perpetually reimagined[2]. And it is not just people who live in a metropolis who have become more globally-minded and mobile. Goods, services and information are also crossing borders with more ease due to increasingly liberal trade policies and greater global information flows enabled by the internet. Where colonialism and capitalism once started this process, digitisation has given it new forms and meanings. As a result, even those living in the most remote villages can access ideas and products from across the globe, which was previously unheard of. So whereas previously, designers and strategists were creating mainly for people just like them, many of today's products and services are falling into the hands of all sorts of different people, spanning Ottawa to Timbuktu. What does all of this mean for global organisations and companies serving the world or wishing to do so?

1   For a good introduction to the forces of globalisation, see: Steger, M. B. (2009). Globalization: A Very Short Introduction. Oxford: Oxford University Press.

2   For further reading on imagined communities and geographies, see: Anderson, Benedict R. O'G. (1991). Imagined communities: Reflections on the origin and spread of nationalism (Revised and extended. ed.). London: Verso; Said, E. [1979] Imaginative Geography and Its Representations: Orientalizing the Oriental. Orientalism. New York: Vintage.

3   Wells, H. G. (1920). The Outline of History. Garden City, New York: Garden City Publishing Co., Inc: https://commons.wikimedia.org/wiki/File:Wells_Reindeer_Age_articles.png

4   Zuckerman, E. (2011) Those White Plastic Chairs – The Monobloc and the Context-Free Object. [digital source] Retrieved from: http://www.ethanzuckerman.com/blog/2011/04/06/those-white-plastic-chairs-the-monobloc-and-the-context-free-object/

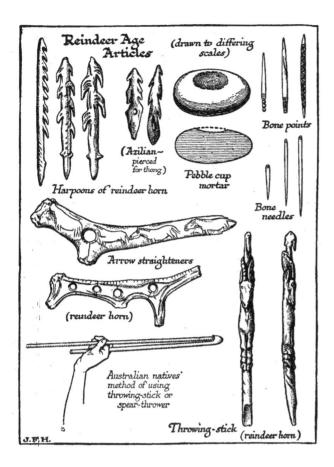

Looking back in time forces us to think about how objects were made, for whom, and why. These ancient hunting tools, as illustrated (top left) in H.G. Wells' 1920 'The Outline of History'[3], were most likely crafted by the same people who used them. In contrast (right) sits the Monobloc chair, which was initially designed in 1946 in Canada by D.C. Simpson and has since been manufactured and sold by the millions around the world. Accordingly, social theorist, Ethan Zuckerman[4], describes it as having achieved a global ubiquity: "The Monobloc is one of the few objects I can think of that is free of any specific context. Seeing a white plastic chair in a photograph offers you no clues about where or when you are."

The role of research in innovation strategy

In many of the organisations we have worked with, we see innovation capacity becoming less Western-centric, and organisations everywhere are now acknowledging the benefits of having distributed design and innovation teams. They are shifting toward more open, networked operating models in order to thrive in the global, networked age. Regardless of the driving factors, opportunities for new or improved products and services can be identified anywhere, and organisations are becoming more aware of this. Opportunities can be small and simple, and lead to needed incremental solutions. They can also be completely disruptive, leading to new meanings and launching organisations into entirely new markets. While more opportunities always seem like a good thing, we see organisations struggling to prioritise which areas to focus on, especially in light of different stakeholder interests and a lack of generally accepted solid justifications. The challenges for designers and product and innovation managers are magnified on a global scale.

Multiple strategies in an Innovation Portfolio

Amidst these difficult decisions, with multiple stakeholders and timelines to cater for, organisations find themselves in need of a way to prioritise areas for focus. Roberto Verganti, in his book "Design-Driven Innovation"[1], proposes a model that organisations can use to analyse their innovation strategies. He outlines three strategies: market-pull innovation, technology-push innovation and design-driven innovation.

Market-Pull Innovation

Market-pull innovation starts with an analysis of user needs and then searches for technologies that can better satisfy them, or else updates product languages to respond to existing trends. User-centred innovation is considered a type of market-pull innovation, as it seeks to better understand and satisfy dominant meanings. These types of innovations are typically informed by user experience and market research and tend to lead to incremental improvements.

Technology-Push Innovation

Technology-push innovation refers to the radical innovation of technologies as a result of advanced research and development projects. These types of innovations lead to radical improvements, disrupt markets and are often the source of long-term competitive advantage.

Design-Driven Innovation

Finally, Verganti outlines design-driven innovation. This strategy builds upon the understanding that people do not just buy products, but also meanings. Of course utility and function are important, but people also use things for profound emotional, psychological and socio-cultural reasons. This is why "firms should look beyond features, functions and performance and understand the real meanings people give to things"[2]. This mindset is especially important at the early stages of innovation, when the idea of the product or service is still being formed. Radical innovation, therefore, stems from radical innovation of meaning. This innovation strategy requires a specific type of research approach and mindset.

Each strategy has its place in an organisation's innovation portfolio, depending on industry type and the level of improvement or change envisioned for the product, product range, or entire strategic direction. Organisations can have multiple products at varying stages along their lifecycle, each demanding a different innovation strategy or combination thereof. We find that Verganti's model provides a helpful way to think about innovation in organisations, and position the research that we do amidst the bigger picture. It is also a nice way to think about the different types of research an organisation can choose to conduct, and how various approaches serve different purposes for different organisational stakeholders.

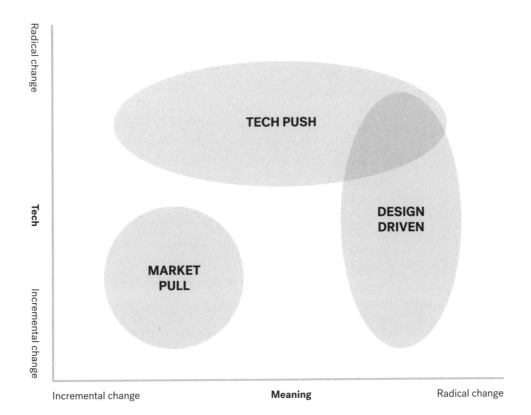

Verganti's model[3] highlights three innovation strategies that organisations can choose to pursue. He proposes that to pursue design-driven innovation, entirely new meanings must be created for existing services or products. As a result they can then even rival technologically superior competitors. The Nintendo Wii, released in 2006, is a good example of the result of design-driven innovation. It radically transformed the meaning of gaming from passive immersion in a virtual world to active, physical entertainment in the physical world.

Different research approaches for different innovation strategies

When we think about the different types of research an organisation can do, a few immediately come to mind: R&D, market research, and user experience (UX) research. These different types of research map nicely onto Verganti's first two innovation strategies, technology-push and market pull innovation. We have found that organisations are now taking a more organised and strategic approach to the early-stage, exploratory research that they do; what we refer to as 'design research' (see the Introduction of this volume). It not only maps well onto the design-driven innovation strategy, but acts as a bridge that interlinks the three approaches.

Radical change

Tech

Incremental change

TECH PUSH

R&D

DESIGN
DRIVEN

DESIGN
RESEARCH

MARKET
PULL

MARKET
& UK
RESEARCH

Incremental change Meaning Radical change

The above diagram illustrates how different types of research support
different innovation strategies, as imposed by STBY on Verganti's model:
'R&D', which is traditionally in-house and technology focused; 'market
and UX research', which involve observation rooms with one-way mirrors
and focus groups; and 'design research', which observes and interacts
with people in the environments where they live and work.

Organisations pursuing a technology-push strategy for a product or product range will, for example, invest heavily in R&D. A team of engineers, or industrial scientists are tasked with either directly developing and testing new products or conducting applied research in scientific or technological fields to facilitate future product development. Investing in the search for breakthrough technologies can lead to quantum leaps in product performance and give organisations long-term competitive advantage. Organisations can choose to do this kind of research in-house, or outsource to universities, government labs or independent R&D organisations.

At the same time, the organisation may also have a mature product in one market that needs different positioning to be successful in another. Here, the organisation will rely on consumer research to inform a different marketing strategy. Again, this research can be done in-house, or outsourced to an external market research agency that reports directly back to the internal marketing team. It could also be that an organisation seeks to incrementally improve a product or a service experience in light of customer feedback — in the case of a software company, for example — and leverage user experience research (also called UX research) to do so. We have seen

a growing number of organisations building internal user research capacity. There are also many agencies who provide various options for companies to outsource such research, under different categories (customer experience, user research, UX, etc.).

Trends toward more integrated product-service systems are blurring the lines between traditional R&D, and early-stage software and service design research. A 2016 PwC report[4] investigating trends at the world's 1000 largest corporate R&D spenders found that most of the world's major innovators are "moving into a new world in which R&D is shifting more and more to developing the software that enables and enhances the performance of their products, and on developing services they can sell along with the products, which provide customers with additional features and improved usability." Formulating this trend as driven by software resonates with Verganti's technology-driven innovation. In STBY's experience, this applies as much to services as to software, which puts the development in a broader context where meaning is as important as technology. Service design is often considered the best, most holistic way to approach innovation through integrated product-service systems.

One of our clients, Philips, illustrates this transition

The 'design squiggle'[6] by Damien Newman represents an innovation process where an area is first explored at the 'fuzzy front end of innovation' before getting to insights, opportunities, ideas and concepts. As the process moves forward, there is no clear or linear path, but rather a path that gets more clear and less messy over time. One of STBY's projects for a water utility company in the UK is a good example. To understand people's experiences with water, our team visited people in their homes to collect stories about anything relating to water. This empathic research catalysed early stage explorations and discussions on opportunity areas as different as school programmes and water bill redesigns.

well. Originally a product -oriented company, Philips has now transitioned to thinking more holistically about the experiences around the interconnected products and services it develops. This shift has also led to a change in the way they think about and organise for innovation. So-called 'experience domains' now provide collective spaces for various organisational units (business strategy, design, marketing, engineering) to explore and develop new meanings in these domains from multiple perspectives[5].

Finally, an organisation could be pursuing radical innovation, looking to create completely new meanings for existing or future products and services. Sometimes this space is referred to as the 'fuzzy front end' of innovation because ideas and propositions are still uncertain and ill-defined. Such a design-driven strategy requires a specific type of research approach and mindset, and it is this space where we position ourselves and much of our design research work.

We acknowledge that these innovation strategies and the research approaches that enable them are not mutually exclusive. In fact, they can be highly interconnected and sometimes overlapping. As previously noted, digitisation and servitisation blur the line between traditional R&D and design-driven innovation research because it forces the more structured worlds of science and engineering to adopt and embrace more agile, open and rapid ways of

working — and vice versa. A mixed bag of strategies in an innovation portfolio naturally requires a mixed bag of research approaches. Design research builds bridges across these different approaches. As organisations become more global, what does this mean for these mixed bags and bridges? More specifically, what are the implications for how organisations structure and empower their people to innovate, both incrementally and radically, on a global scale?

1   Verganti, R. (2009). Design-Driven Innovation: changing the rules of competition by radically innovating what things mean. Boston, MA: Harvard Business Press.
2   Ibid. p. 4.
3   Ibid. p. 55.
4   PwC. (2006). Global Innovation 1000 Study. Retrieved: 3 Apr. 2017 from https://www.strategyand.pwc.com/innovation1000
5   Deckers, E., Gardien, P. (2015). Experience Domains for Common Ground. In: "THIS IS CRISP". CRISP magazine vol.5 2015: 32. Retrieved 3 May 2017 from: http://www. crisprepository.nl/_uploaded/O-from-CRISP-magazine5.pdf
6   Newman, D. The Process of Design Squiggle. Central Office of Design. Retrieved from: http://cargocollective.com/central/ The-Design-Squiggle

Organising for global innovation

How are the organisations preparing themselves for innovation and research going global? We have found that much of what has been written about innovation (and the research that enables it) tends to focus on market-pull and technology-push strategies. There are extensive reports and articles that analyse how companies have organised their market research and R&D capabilities in light of globalisation, but there is not yet much literature on how design research enables a more human-centred and design-driven approach to global innovation. Given the interconnectedness of the innovation strategies, we find traces of design research across the global innovation portfolio.

Design research and global market–pull innovation

Access to the global marketplace is shaking up the perception of marketing's strategic importance and the way in which organisations are rethinking marketing in terms of structure, ways of working, purpose and capacity. A 2014 Harvard Business Review article[1] outlines what makes the "Ultimate Marketing Machine", based on in-depth qualitative interviews with 350 CEOs, CMOs and agency heads worldwide, in addition to 10,000 quantitative surveys from 92 countries. By a wide margin, respondents in overperforming companies agreed with the statements "Local marketing understands the global strategy" and "Global marketing understands the local marketing reality".

Naghi and Para (2013: 172) similarly write about the influence of globalisation on marketing activities and the market research process[2]. For organisations with developed products and services (i.e. most companies), being strategic about differences and similarities in price, promotion, and distribution in different global locations is key. This global-local understanding stems from a few key drivers, including a strong global vision and brand purpose, a networked structure, agile cross-functional teams and the continual building of internal capabilities.

Increasingly, companies are looking to enhance the value of their products by thinking more about customer experiences. With the trends of digitisation previously noted, organisations must understand not just how people feel about products and brands, but how they *experience* them across numerous physical and digital touchpoints. These trends have led to a growth in the field of User Experience (UX) design and research. Although this type of research is also under the umbrella of the market-pull innovation strategy, UX research is more focused on how a person uses or experiences a product, not on what they may or may not buy.

As companies become more global, and users become more internationally dispersed, understanding similarities and differences in how people use products across markets is also increasingly vital. Our friend and colleague, Dan Szuc of agency Apogee in Hong Kong, has written extensively on the topic of global UX design and research. He has noted a number of ways that companies manage UX design and research in light of global growth. These strategies are influenced by different management strategies[3]:

One product: a product is designed for a home market and sold globally with only minor localisation.

Local control: although under a global brand, each product is really a franchise in its own market, and makes its own design decisions.

Global templates with local variations: a global UX group creates and manages a set of templates that set a global standard and allow for local adaptations.

Companies can have different global growth and brand management strategies, which influence the way that they may go about global UX research. Depending on internal capacity and resources, organisations can choose to conduct overseas UX research themselves. More often, organisations will work with local research agencies who are more sensitive to appropriate research methods, customs and culture. For multi-site global work, multiple vendors in each respective location are selected to support a global research project.

While global market research and UX research are informing global market-pull innovation strategies, companies are also adapting R&D capabilities to stimulate technology-push innovation on a global scale.

Design research and global technology-push innovation

A notable 2006 report by Booz & Co and INSEAD[4] maps how, as companies have fanned out across the globe to access the potential of new markets, their R&D activity has become more international or dispersed in character. This dispersion is not equal across the globe, and differs based on the organisation's home region, and on the industry type. They found that companies based in Western Europe are most dispersed in terms of R&D and that sectors that rely more heavily on complex knowledge that is difficult to move had less dispersed innovation footprints: Pharmaceuticals and Healthcare, Industrial Manufacturing, Energy and Utilities, and Consumer Goods all produced low scores in terms of R&D dispersion. The report also analyses how the drivers behind R&D internationalisation have been changing in response to the increasing dispersion of knowledge (with new centres of competence emerging in what were previously unlikely places) and industry convergence, and what this means for organisations. It concludes with the finding that whilst many companies are building more international R&D networks, few have really begun to build the internal capabilities to run these networks effectively and efficiently.

The report is also notable in that it distinguishes between organisations that rely mostly on complex knowledge, and those that rely mostly on codified knowledge, ie. explicit knowledge that can be readily articulated, accessed and verbalized. Codified knowledge can be easily transmitted to others. By complex knowledge, the authors refer to knowledge that is "embedded in a local context and which requires a level of 'seeing and doing' as it is very difficult to articulate". This type of knowledge is of key importance in the service sector. As servitisation[5], fuelled by digitisation, becomes a trend, this distinction is becoming increasingly important. Manufacturing companies embracing a service orientation, develop more and better services with the aim to satisfy customer's needs, achieve competitive advantages and enhance firm performance. Organisations developing the capabilities they need to provide services and solutions that supplement their traditional product offerings must match that capability with more interconnected strategy-making and research capacity. Traditional understandings of R&D make no distinction between manufacturing and

service-sector R&D, and therefore fall short in this regard.

Technological breakthroughs are no doubt important for organisations seeking radical change but this does not mean that they must develop these technological innovations themselves. Many are already available on the market, ready to integrate in new products or services. However, without the understanding of the interplay between technical breakthroughs and the development of new meanings for products and experiences, organisations will lag behind. Indeed, the report identifies that "whilst finding new knowledge is not seen as a significant challenge, companies face serious difficulties in assessing the value of new knowledge." This increasingly recognised necessity has perhaps fuelled the recent increased interest around exploratory research and design-thinking; they have provided a language, mindset and methodological toolkit to bridge organisational silos and help people collaborate in innovation efforts (see the chapter on Practice).

Design research and global design-driven innovation

For design-driven innovation of products and services, organisations must seek to understand meaning rather than market or function. As a result, the focus is on the interpretation of culture instead of the discovery of laws through experimental science, as technology cognitive psychology require. Anthropology and social sciences like cultural studies tend to offer the best methodologies and frameworks to investigate meaning. Social scientist and anthropologist Clifford Geertz[6] was an early advocate of using an interpretive approach in ethnography, and his ideas are still influential today. He sees reality as something that is achieved by people, and not something by which people are ruled. Through creating meaning, people achieve social order. Global design research, which needs to take into account cultural differences and similarities, is generally based on this thinking.

The interpretative approach requires an open, collaborative organisation of innovation in organisations. After all, the results of any such research will not be indisputable facts, but interpretations that can be contested. This should be seen as a positive characteristic because "progress is marked less by a perfection of consensus than by a refinement of debate. What gets better is the precision with which we vex each other"[7], Geertz wrote. Such debates are not uncommon in companies and other organisations' innovation teams either. They are however often experienced as a burden rather than a blessing, and tend to slow things down. This need not be as we experienced in developing the Practice of Good Reason (see the previous chapter).

Ethnography, including when it is deployed in global design research and innovation, is best understood as a dialogue that continually flows. Design research that takes an ethnographic approach differs therefore from market research, UX research and R&D in that it does not deliver facts but instead interpretations and debate. This has fundamental consequences for how to organise such research and how to operate as an organisation to make design-driven innovation a success. Interpretation and

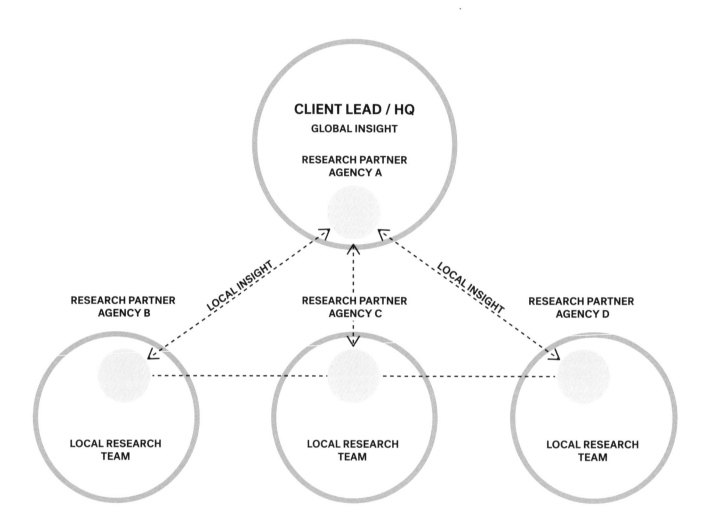

The lead-organisation network partner model: For global design research projects, dispersed client teams and research agencies work together with a shared overarching research plan and guidelines. They are 'orchestrated' by a lead agency and a client lead. Local insights across research locations are shared and analysed on a global scale.

debate require a range people, disciplines and silos to be involved in the creation of meaning. It is not possible for one small research group to create that meaning through interpretation and then impose it on others as if it were a fact in a report.

The exploratory nature of design-driven innovation is an essential contribution to the fuzzy front end of innovation, before new offerings are even conceived. Increasingly, we see more of an appetite for this type of innovation and the exploratory, yet actionable, research that fuels it on a global scale. We are particularly interested in this area because it is where we find that our clients often struggle the most. With many moving parts and targets scattered across the globe, and the need to keep a dialogue on meaning flowing, early-stage exploration requires a fine balance between openness and agility on the one hand, and structure, direction and precision on the other. The rise in the importance of network structures, inter-disciplinary teams, agility, globally-minded people and internal capacity-building resonates well with creating knowledge through dialogues and interpretation, as we do in conducting global design research projects with clients.

Although there is not much written about it, we do know that early-stage global design research is indeed taking place (under many different names). We have played an active role ourselves in supporting client organisations undertaking design research over the years. In doing so, we have reflected upon a number of ways of working that facilitate early-stage innovation projects and the types of collaborations that enable them.

For many of our projects, we have embraced networked ways of working to support our clients (as outlined in the chapter Networks). Global organisations are, by nature, network organisations, although some are more flat and interconnected than others. For global design research projects, especially those that involve multiple locations, it means that organisations must often work with many different research partners to conduct fieldwork in different locations. Relatedly, because design research typically happens in the very early stages of product and service development, its results are relevant to many organisational stakeholders who either need to be part of the ongoing dialogue or be able to trace the evidence on which the interpretations are based. Through our own experience we have therefore found that global design research benefits from being collaborative. This implies interconnectedness between the internal client stakeholders who reap the benefits of the research, interconnectedness between the researchers across the globe, and close interaction between client stakeholders and the research process. This is one of the reasons why the Reach Network operating model evolved as it did — as an inclusive way to provide more joined-up design research on a global scale.

In the case of our global research projects with the Reach Network, we typically work with clients in a 'lead-organisation network partner model'. This model provides relatively centralised control and management of the research process, while allowing for the flexibility needed for local partners to adapt research methods to their local context. The lead-organisation model also streamlines and standardises documentation and analysis of actionable insights and opportunities for new product and service concepts on a global scale, whilst keeping everything flexible enough to allow for meaningful, necessary local appropriations. For projects that are by nature uncertain and exploratory, it is important to enable this flexible, yet structured and actionable, approach. It is also important in creating a global curated repository of design research and insights (libraries of evidence) that multiple stakeholders can tap into as different business problems arise on a global scale and a solid evidence base for collaborative interpretation is required (touched upon in the chapter Practice).

The composition of global and local client teams varies from project to project. Typically, the client lead will be based in the headquarters and one or more of the main regional offices may be involved. The client lead and the lead research agency together craft the overall research objectives, scope and plan. Local research teams are engaged in chosen locations. They detail the approach to suit the various local contexts, in order to achieve the shared research objectives. The local fieldwork team may include stakeholders from the local or regional client team, if the organisation has a presence in the location where the research is being conducted. In other cases, members of the client organisation may travel to participate in fieldwork alongside the local research agency. In this way of working, the client and agency teams are mirroring each other's organisation as a network with a lead to coordinate and connect efforts. This ensures a good balance between structure and flexibility.

Orchestration as a practical organising principle and mindset

Rigid structures and organisational charts are ill-suited to global explorations involving many different moving parts that interact over time. This type of work requires agile network structures and flexible yet visionary management techniques and mindsets. We have come to use the metaphor of orchestration to describe how to organise and manage such complex projects and constellations of people.[8]

Perhaps most important is the understanding that with global explorations, just as with music, there are many different styles of orchestration. Some of the case studies throughout this publication illustrate these different styles, and there are no doubt many more, dependant on the conductor, musicians, musical instruments, scores and audience involved. Orchestration should be seen as a balancing act, rather than a process, involving various activities. These include building common ground, building involvement in the global team, steering process to keep making progress, and finally navigation to give everyone the same sense of direction of where the project is going. Orchestration happens at the network level; it contains practical macro-management principles that help create a shared mindset, across multiple micro-level activities in different localities.

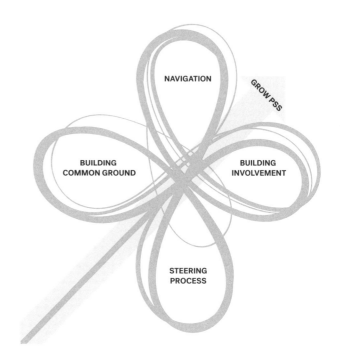

The idea of thinking about orchestration as a
way of managing complex projects emerged from
a study on the development of product-service
systems (PSSs). Orchestration[9] entails four
connected principles: Building common ground;
Building involvement; Steering processes; and
Navigating. These are all activities in themselves
and orchestration is the activity that keeps these
other four moving, connected, and in balance.
STBY orchestrates parts of projects for clients
regularly, which includes situations in workshops
as much as in between meetings, online and offline.

1   de Swaan Arons, M., van den Driest, F., Weed, K. (2014).
    The Ultimate Marketing Machine. Harvard Business Review,
    July-August: Retrieved 3 May 2017 from: https://hbr.
    org/2014/07/the-ultimate-marketing-machine
2   Naghi, R., Para, I. (2013). The Effects Of Globalization On
    Marketing. GSTF Journal on Business Review 2.3: pp. 168-173.
3   As outlined in Quesenbery, W., Szuc, D. (2012). Global UX.
    1st ed. Waltham, MA: Morgan Kaufmann. Print.
4   Doz, Y., Wilson, K., Veldhoen, S., Goldbrunner, T., Altman, G.
    (2006). Innovation: Is Global The Way Forward? Booz Allen
    Hamilton, INSEAD.

5   Ren, G., Gregory, M.J. (2007). Servitization in manufacturing
    companies: a conceptualization, critical review, and research
    agenda. In: Frontiers in Service Conference 2007, 2007-10-4
    to 2007-10-7, San Francisco, CA, US.
6   Geertz, C. (1973). The Interpretation of Cultures. New York,
    Basic Books.
7   Ibid., p.29.
8   For further thoughts on 'Orchestration' see: Raijmakers, B.,
    Vervloed, J., Jan Wierda, K. (2015). Orchestration. CRISP
    Magazine n.5 2015: 24-33.
9   Ibid, p. 24.

Diverse and changing landscapes

In thinking, talking and writing about innovation in organisations, it is easy to put everyone in the same bucket. But there are important and significant distinctions across different sectors and industries (e.g. for-profit vs. non-profit, automotive, consumer, electronics, finance etc.), which influence the composition of innovation portfolios and the organisation of global (and local) innovation capacity. One size does not necessarily fit all, as already alluded to with the orchestration metaphor, in light of different strategic and financial constraints.

As providers of global design research, it is important for us and our network partners to also be sensitive to the different innovation barriers in each of these organisation types. We find that public and non-profit organisations, understandably, tend to value accountability to public and integrity over innovation and creativity. This baseline value can sometimes create less fertile environments for design research and the creative methods that it employs. Yet, as many non-governmental organisations expand their operations overseas, efforts to re-examine and reframe[1] problem areas and re-evaluate offerings in light of deeper understanding of human context are perhaps more important than ever before. Recent discussions with those working in this sector hint that this view is becoming more recognised by high-level decision makers in these organisations.

For-profit organisations often face a different opposition to innovation. Operational excellence can be a dominant force in companies, and needs fixed structures and ways of operating. That is why companies set their innovation efforts often outside their normal operation. This solves the problem only temporarily, as organisation must then integrate successful innovation later into the mainstream organisation. Either way, the consequence is that successful innovation not only creates new products and services, but also new ways to operate and relate to each other in organisations, which poses a set of challenges in itself.

Also, across for-profit organisations we have seen notable differences in familiarity with and appetite for design research. Within many organisations there are a few 'champions' for the design research approach, but others may need to be coached in understanding and embracing the methods and mindset. This has made us think more about how we can support capacity building within organisations as we work with clients to conduct design research. For global organisations, this has meant developing global coaching and training toolkits and programmes. This is a recent development for STBY and the Reach Network, and one that we are excited about moving forward.

We see these internal champions within client organisations as 'co-pioneers'. And because our design research process is extremely open and collaborative, talking about our practice and developing new exploratory methods with them has helped us reflect upon how early-stage exploratory research can connect the dots in global organisations. As organisations grow and expand overseas, this creates more uncertainty for organisational stakeholders. Providing not just global and local understanding, but also help with developing the right mindset, support and structures, we feel that global design research can play an important role in guiding organisations in a global, networked world where local and global cultures are a continuous flow of meaning created by people.

1   Dorst, Kees. (2015). Frame Innovation: Create New Thinking
     by Design. MIT press; and Dorst, K. (2016). Designing for Good.
     Bis B.V., Uitgeverij, BIS Publishers.

OUR GLOBAL DESIGN RESEARCH MANIFESTO

On people, culture, and the world

People live in a global world. Many of us share the internet, we travel, and companies create global products and services. We are all connected in many ways.

People are all human, with human needs, ambitions, flaws, and achievements. That doesn't mean we are all the same though. Being different is human too.

Reality is achieved by people. We 'spin webs of significance' that together form our culture. Empathic interpretation is needed to understand what matters to us people.

On what drives and motivates us as global design researchers

We believe in deep cultural sensitivity rather than superficial skills that can easily be transferred. We analyse through interpretation and 'thick description' rather than simply applying models.

We value deep cultural experience and expertise, as we need to step into the shoes of our research participants, and observe the context they live and work in.

On how we operate as global design researchers

We look for relevant global similarities; often already implicitly existing, or to be further enhanced, as long as they are understandable and acceptable for most people.

We look for meaningful local differences that matter to both people and organisations. There is no point in detailed findings that would in fact not really make much meaningful difference.

We make the familiar strange, by taking a step back from everyday life. Being familiar with life in several countries and cultures helps, as it makes the culture one grew up in less obvious.

We make the strange familiar through working with local peers in different cultures. We all live in different places and have different cultural backgrounds, experiences and upbringings. We call upon each other to make the strange familiar.

On how we relate to others in our work

We work in the context of human-centred design. After all, we are all human: the participants in our global design research, our clients and we ourselves.

We collaborate closely with our clients, because they need to work with and own the results. We do fieldwork together, and engage in joint workshops to make sense together.

We keep people present through their stories. People's stories provide the inspiration and evidence that power change and innovation, again and again, every time.

Image credits

All images by STBY or Reach
partners, unless otherwise noted.

p.4
NASA/JPL. (1996). *Voyager 1*
[digital image]. Retrieved from:
https://photojournal.jpl.nasa.gov/
catalog/PIA00452

Introduction
p.9
Dreyfuss, H. (1960). *The Measure
of Man: Human Factors in Design*.
New York: Whitney Library of Design.

p.10
Photo by Apogee, Hong Kong.

Networks
p.25
All photos by Apogee, Hong Kong.

p.27
All photos by Matchboxology, Cape
Town, South Africa.

p.29
All photos by Quicksand, New Delhi,
India.

p.30
All stills from a video by fuelfor,
Singapore.

p.32
Top two photos by Deutsche
Telekom AG.

p.34
All photos by Apogee, Hong Kong,
except bottom left photo by Quicksand,
New Delhi, India.

p.38
Photo by Quicksand, New Delhi, India.

p.39
Innovation Spiral by Nesta, London,
UK. DIY toolkit:
http://diytoolkit.org/background/

Practice
p.48
Photo (top) by Kat Gough.

Photo (bottom left) by Michael Davis
Burchat.

p.49
Photo (bottom left) by Michael Davis
Burchat.

p.51
Photo (bottom left) by Kat Gough.

p.70
Photo (top left) by Kat Gough.

p.74
Photo (bottom left) by Kat Gough.

p.80
Photo by Lili Davis Burchat.

Landscapes
p.83
Wells, H. G. (1920). *The Outline
of History*. Garden City, New York:
Garden City Publishing Co., Inc:
https://commons.wikimedia.org/wiki/
File:Wells_Reindeer_Age_articles.png

p.85
Berglund J. (2006). *Wii* [digital image].
Retrieved from: https://www.flickr.com/
photos/tyrian123/338189392/

My Nintendo News. *Nintendo Wii*
[digital image]. Retrieved from:
https://mynintendonews.
com/2011/05/06/nintendo-wii-
stroke-patient-attributes-her-recovery-
to-the-nintendo-wii/

p.86
QIAGEN. (2011). *Application laboratory
with QIAsymphony* [digital image].
Retrieved from: https://www.flickr.com/
photos/qiagen/7690580838/

Addison, B. (2009). *University
of Baltimore usability testing lab*
[digital image]. Retrieved from:
https://www.flickr.com/photos/
add1sun/3312538837/in/
photostream/